The Development
of Foster City

The Development of Foster City

of Foster City

T. Jack Foster, Jr.

To order additional copies of this book, contact:
Xlibris Corporation
1-888-795-4274
www.Xlibris.com
Orders@Xlibris.com
118054

CONTENTS

Snapshot of partners standing in the hayfield of Brewer Island.
The levee can be seen in the background.
From left: Richard H. Foster, T. Jack Foster, T. Jack Foster, Jr.
and John R. (Bob) Foster.

CHAPTER ONE

The Times

THERE ARE MANY things about the development of Foster City where it helps to understand the 1960's. In the international situation, the cold war was at its hottest (coldest?). There was the Berlin Wall, the Cuban missile crisis, and problems brewing in Vietnam. In the United States, times were good and money was cheap. In California, growth was what everybody wanted and Governor Pat Brown proudly announced that California had passed New York State in population, then about 20 million in each state. Coldwell Banker's logo showed the silhouette of a city skyline with black smoke belching from the smoke stacks, suggesting vitality and vigor. The civil rights movement was building as was the environmental movement.

The State Highway Department had adopted an aggressive and ambitious master plan to accommodate the traffic needs of a growing state. All planning bodies were expected to honor it. Highway 92 was planned to be the "Sierras to the Sea Freeway" running from the Sierras to Half Moon Bay. The master plan called for a "Bayfront Freeway," built on combinations of fill and bridges, paralleling Bayshore Freeway and running just off shore of Foster City to the east. Both freeways impacted Foster City planning.

Locally, the attitude was pro growth. It was not even a debate issue. In 1959 the San Mateo County master plan projected Brewer Island, which became Foster City, as being all residential with a potential 60,000 people. The school districts were worried that such a population would bring down the assessed valuation behind each school child and thereby create a large financial problem. Brewer Island was two thirds in the San Mateo Elementary School District and San Mateo High School District and one third in the Belmont Elementary School District and Sequoia High School District. This could have been a serious problem for the planners in designing the schools into the land plan.

The general philosophy which prevailed at the time, in regard to development, was that vacant land which had been on the tax roll from the outset and had received little or none of the benefits of the taxing entities, was fully entitled to be used by the owner. Of course there were planning commissions and zoning laws, but, unlike today, no question of whether or not the land could be used. Furthermore, as it came into use, it was entitled to the same benefits and services that it would have received had it always been used. It was entitled to police and fire protection, to schools, to parks and recreation. And the owner of that land *did not have to pay for those entitlements!!* The attitude was that he or she had already paid for those services by virtue of having paid taxes since the creation of the taxing entity and would continue to pay along with everybody else.

In time, the philosophy changed so that the developer of such a parcel had to pay fees to cover those previously "free" entitlements, and to provide whatever lands are needed, and in some cases to build whatever public buildings are needed to service that community, including schools, parks, fire stations, etc. They would have to "buy in" to the community, not unlike an initiation fee to a country club. But that was not the rule when Foster City was being developed.

Finally, consider the change in the value of the dollar. From 1960 to 2012, the cost of living has increased about seven and a half times. When I write that we paid $13 million for the land, consider that that is the equivalent of $97 million today. Residential real estate has inflated more than that. The first houses that sold in Foster City were priced at $23,000. Based on the dollar, that would be $172,000 in 2012. Homes are worth many times that.

CHAPTER TWO

The Start

IT WAS 1958 when my father, T. Jack Foster, my brothers and I first saw Brewer Island, the place that would eventually become Foster City. Dad was living most of the time in Pebble Beach, though the home office of our family partnership, T. Jack Foster & Sons, was in Oklahoma City where it had always been. The company previous to that was Likins Foster & Associates. When Dad bought out the Bill Likins interest in 1955, he changed the name to reflect the new family partnership but kept the home office and the staff where it was. I was living in Hawaii where I was in charge of our activities, consisting of developing and selling some 1500 houses and processing for construction the 25 story Foster Tower Hotel in Waikiki. Brother Bob (John R. Foster) lived in Oklahoma City where he looked after the family oil interests. Dick (Richard H. Foster) was in El Paso, Texas, building a 450 unit apartment project, another family investment.

Dad called us all to meet in California. The purpose, he said, was to look over the Northern California real estate market to see if there was a development project that we might want to take on—one that we could all work together on. I am not sure he thought we would find one or if it was just a good excuse for all of us to get together. In any event, as happens in family businesses, the motivation was not entirely economically motivated, whether it was to be togetherness on the short term, as we looked, or long term if we found something and chose to buy in.

We looked at parcels and potential development opportunities from Sacramento to San Jose. In San Mateo we met a developer by the name of Richard Grant who showed us Brewer Island. We were very impressed with what we saw.

Grant's office was on Norfolk Street in San Mateo and from his office we could see across the lagoon the levee which surrounded this remarkable land area. Beyond the levee were high power electric transmission lines of various sizes running generally north and south. We could see a barn in the distance and, beyond that, the towers of the lift section of the San Mateo-Hayward bridge. Being at a level lower than the levee, we could see little else.

There were seven of us: four Fosters, Grant, an associate of Grant's, and Bill Innes, an executive in the Foster partnership. Taking two cars, we drove to Third Avenue in San Mateo and turned eastward onto the two lane approach road to San Mateo-Hayward bridge. We crossed a curving bridge over a drainage outlet to the bay and onto a roadway which was positioned on top of the levee. From that vantage, being appreciably higher than the land below, we saw for the first time the hay field and the vast land area that was Brewer Island. As our cars approached the toll station which was then on the west end of the bridge, we turned off through a gate down into the meadow where the dirt road divided into different directions. We then took a left turn which took us up onto the eastern levee where we proceeded slowly in a southerly direction on the rutted road, gazing over the land below.

Here was a vast meadow, 3000 acres, over four square miles, completely flat and not a tree on it. It was strategically located in the San Francisco Bay area and separated from the "mainland" by the waterway which we had seen behind Grant's office. The waterway was called Marina Lagoon (formerly known as Seal Slough, named for the seals that lived there in better environmental days.)

We learned that the island resulted from the efforts of a farmer by the name of Frank Brewer who, in 1900, built levees in the mud flats so to create land for a meadow for the grazing of dairy cattle. He used an assessment bond proceeding to borrow the money for the cost. With the sunny dry summers and the spring and summer winds for which the Bay area is known, the area within the new levees dried in a short few years and was put into cultivation for hay. In our subsequent investigation as to the impact of the 1906 earthquake on the levees, we learned that the new levees survived the quake without damage but it scared the cows and knocked some bales of hay out of the loft of the barn.

This land was not for sale. 2700 acres of it was owned by the Schilling family who lived in Woodside. The other 300 acres was owned by a dairyman named Thomas Therkildsen. It was his barn that we could see. About one third of the Schilling interest was actually owned by the Leslie Salt Company which also owned thousands of acres adjacent to the Bay from Brewer Island south and up the other side of the Bay. Its business was the manufacture of salt by the evaporation process, and the evaporating ponds started on the southern portion of Brewer Island. As the salinity increased with evaporation, the brine was pumped to similar ponds southward until it reached Redwood City where the "harvesting" took place. The Schilling family owned the Leslie Salt Company.

This is the same family that, in earlier generations, owned Schilling Tea and Spices, which was sold to the McCormick Corporation. They got back into the spice business through their Leslie Salt Company's ownership of Spice Islands. Leslie Salt Company was eventually sold to the Cargill Company and the salt operation together with the vast land holding around the edge of the Bay went to that large family owned company.

Richard Grant, who lived in Woodside, had a good relationship with the Schillings, having purchased from them the land which he developed into Parkside in San Mateo. It was August Schilling who he knew and with whom he had dealt. Grant felt that an approach to him might result in the family's interest in selling the land. Such a meeting was held, and August Schilling and my father hit it off very well. Mr. Schilling was noncommittal at first but allowed that the family might be interested in a transaction. There was no effort being made by the family to sell the property, and he allowed that he would welcome further discussion on the matter. While no option or right of refusal was offered or requested, my father was encouraged to continue his investigation.

Was there interest on our part? There certainly was, particularly from my brothers and me. Dad's greater experience told him instinctively that this was no small project. In fact it was huge. But our enthusiasm infected him as well, and he suggested that even without a hold on the property of any kind we spend some money investigating the prospects of developing the land.

Grant's experience and knowledge was a great help and he introduced us to the local civil engineering firm, Wilsey, Ham & Blair, and to the San Francisco soils engineering firm of Dames & Moore. Wilsey, Ham & Blair were the preeminent civil engineers in San Mateo County, widely respected by local authorities. Dames & Moore were the preeminent international engineers in earth sciences, with offices all over the world. We were fortunate in that that firm was based in San Francisco and directed by the founder, Bill Moore. Their ability and integrity was such that their involvement ensured approval by F.H.A. and others who might be called upon for a financial participation of some kind.

We decided to spend $75,000 to investigate the development potential. The primary interest was basic engineering feasibility, but our investigation included legal title research and examination of California bond assessment procedures.

The biggest surprise was when we learned the reason that the land was vacant: that this land was formerly tidal marsh, that the levees that protected it from the Bay were built around 1900 and the drying out process which occurred over the intervening years as the land was put into cultivation only extended down a few feet, and below that was mud for a depth of 60 to 90 feet! The general consensus was that the land could not be developed. But the engineers and Dick Grant thought differently.

One day, my Dad said to Bill Moore, of Dames & Moore, that he wanted a tour of the Bay area to see every bad example of construction on soft soil. We started one morning and spent the entire day driving around the Bay, stopping at several badly designed buildings that had failed as a result of differential settlement. This is a term that means that the land is settling under the weight of the building at different rates. We saw a market with no structural support in the floor. The heavy food bins were sinking, with concrete blocks placed under them to keep them level. The building was weeks from abandonment.

He also showed us some very satisfactory buildings built on the same type of soil performing beautifully. I remember seeing a warehouse where differential settlement was anticipated and the designers chose to accommodate it by creating weak sections in the slab which would allow the building to bend rather than break. At the wall sections, a void was created where they abutted one another, and flashing was installed on both the inside and the outside and as one wall tilted toward or away from the other, it slipped behind the flashing so was irrelevant. Even the gutters were designed to slip smoothly rather than break as one section of the building tipped slightly away from or toward another section.

This was the first example that I had seen of allowing for and designing for differential settlement so that the building was not compromised in any way. We learned early that the answer to building on soft soil was to design thoughtfully and, of equal importance, to ensure that the construction follow the design. We knew that one failure could create a public relations nightmare for the entire project.

At the same time, Wilsey, Ham & Blair was looking at other needs. First and foremost was the problem of drainage. The land was behind levees — the water that fell on it stayed on it until it evaporated. Clearly the land had to be drained. The most economical drainage solution involved placing a minimum of 18 million cubic yards of earth fill! A subsequent chapter describes the fill needs and solution.

The only water that was available was owned by the San Francisco Water Department and its main line from the Hetch Hetchy system was in upper Hillsborough. The important fact was that it was available.

There were no sewer facilities available so a treatment system serving the entire island would have to be built.

Access to the island was poor, being the two lane road on Third Avenue in San Mateo, the access to the San Mateo Hayward Bridge. The general plan for the region called for a "Sierra to the Sea" freeway extending from the Sierra Mountains over the San Mateo Hayward Bridge all the way to Half Moon Bay via the Nineteenth Avenue interchange with Bayshore Freeway. This access was a long time in the future, with no certainty that it would ever be built. Finally, it was built as Highway 92, the J. Arthur Younger Freeway, but did not extend either to the Sierras or to the Sea, but eventually became a valuable access point to Foster City.

The only other potential access points to Foster City were at the Hillsdale/Bayshore and the Ralston/Bayshore interchanges.

Our research told us that the project would be difficult, but nothing told us that it could not be done. With that conclusion, we approached Schilling with a request for a price and an option. A purchase contract was negotiated with the Schilling Estate Company which included the Leslie Salt Company as a seller as to their acreage. With the option in hand, costing $200,000, we accelerated our research efforts and were enabled to approach the County Government and other authorities which had jurisdiction over the project.

As we went more and more public with the concept of developing Brewer Island, we found much enthusiasm, little resistance, and some amount of skepticism. The County Board of Supervisors was enthusiastic. County Manager Bob Stallings was supportive. The County planning department and planning commission were favorable. There were some negative rumblings in the City of San Mateo, mainly reflecting concern that the local school districts would be unduly burdened. There were no environmental concerns raised, mainly because the environmental movement had not started.

After Foster City was under way, the Save the Bay environmental movement started, resulting in the creation of the BCDC (Bay Conservation and Development Commission.) This was by act of the legislature (McAteer-Petris Act) and as the bill was under consideration, Senator Richard Dolwig of San Mateo County, asked the County supervisors for their reaction to the legislation. As chairman of the powerful rules committee in the State Senate, Dolwig controlled what bills came to the floor for action. Since the County had jurisdiction of land use, the supervisors were not anxious to relinquish control to a new state commission whose objectives were different from that of the County's. We also were concerned also about the imposition of another level of control of the development, particularly one whose purpose was to "protect the Bay." In response, Dolwig kept the legislation in the rules committee until it was amended to specifically exclude the lands of Foster City. Once satisfied, Dolwig released the bill from committee. It passed the legislature and was signed into law by the governor in 1965. A spokesman for the Sierra Club said in celebration of the creation of the BCDC, "We were too late to stop Foster City but we'll see that there are no others." He was only slightly wrong; the land which became Redwood Shores was "grandfathered" from the act as was Foster City.

Liking our reception at the County level, we decided that if we were to go forward, we would do so under County jurisdiction. The decision to seek annexation to the City of San Mateo or to incorporate could be made later.

Knowing that we were investigating financing the improvements with some form of assessment proceedings allowed under State law, the Board of Supervisors suggested that we seek passage of an act creating a special district. It would have the same authority of certain water and sewer districts but with additional powers, similar to a City, like police, fire, and park departments. There would be an advantage by having it all under a single jurisdiction. Furthermore, a multiplicity of districts covering differing areas and differing functions would be a burden on County Government which would have to manage them. One significant power of the proposed district was the power to reclaim land, which covered the creation of the lagoons and the filling of the land.

We were referred to Earnest Wilson, attorney in San Mateo specializing in assessment bonding proceedings who had drafted two acts similar to what the Board of Supervisors were recommending for Foster City. He drafted what became Senate Bill 51 creating the Estero Municipal Improvement District It was introduced in the State Senate by Senator Richard Dolwig and in the Assembly by Assemblyman Carl A. (Ike) Britschgi. The support for this legislation came from the County Board of Supervisors who instructed their lobbyist in Sacramento to seek its approval. The bill passed both houses and went to Governor Pat Brown's desk for approval.

Governor Brown demurred for a time, questioning the wisdom of such all-encompassing legislation. Finally, he signed it and it became law. While waiting for the Governor's decision on the matter, my father decided that if it were not signed he would drop the option. Having concluded that all the many difficult problems could be solved, this then became the critical factor which would decide if Foster City went forward.

The Republic National Bank of Dallas, Texas, had been my father's bank for several years. The lines of credit extended to him were more of the conventional type: a secured land and development loan providing there was a "take out" of some sort. A "take out" is a foreseeable means of paying off the loan, with either another loan or through a foreseeable rate of sales.

Foster City represented something entirely different: an enormous venture that would take years to work out. It fit no pattern that the bank had ever done. My father presented it to Fred Florence, the chairman, and

Jim Aston, the president. His enthusiasm was contagious and Mr. Florence said that they would figure a way to do the deal.

The other thing that needed doing prior to going forward was to deal with Dick Grant. He was the local developer with the experience and the contacts and who knew August Schilling. While Grant brought a lot of ability to the table, there was no great financial strength. My father made it clear that he did not want a partner in the venture but he acknowledged that Grant was entitled to compensation for his efforts and for remaining on board to help with the development. The deal which they made was that Grant would be paid a fixed sum for each lot or acre which was sold. He would be paid only out of cash as received, and if acreage was deeded without compensation, he would cooperate but would receive nothing for it. It was designed to eliminate any sort of cash flow problem for the project. He would be limited to a total of $3 million with no time limit, no interest, and no guarantee that that figure would be reached, though we all were confident that it would.

As the development got under way, payments were made to Grant as called for and the relationship was excellent. However, in another matter unrelated to Foster City, Grant was sued by some partners who claimed that their agreement with Grant required that they share in anything that he did. He lost the lawsuit and in collecting on the sizable judgment, his creditors took most of his assets including possession of the $3 million compensation agreement on Foster City. For us it meant the substitution of an unfriendly contractual relationship for a friendly one. For Grant, it ruined him and, in my opinion, led to the breakup of his marriage and an early death.

Our purchase option provided that it be exercised on August 18, 1960, at which time a down payment of $2,413,645 would be made and a note made for the balance. The $10,468,225 debt was to be secured by the land being purchased. Some land was left free and clear of debt. A release price was negotiated. The total purchase price was $12,881,870.

Another item of business: anticipating that we would successfully solve the fill problem and hoping to carry that solution to another opportunity, we asked for and were granted another option from Leslie Salt Company on the 1200 acres south of Brewer Island. In time, with enough to handle in Foster City, we allowed that option to lapse. Subsequently, Leslie Salt formed its own subsidiary, Leslie Properties, and started the development of Redwood Shores on that site. It did not go well for them and they ultimately tendered it to Bank of America in lieu of foreclosure. Bank of America then sold it to a subsidiary of Mobil Oil Company who continued the development.

Governor Pat Brown signed the Estero Bill, so it became apparent for several weeks before the August 1960 option date that we were going to exercise the option so we started to mobilize for the development. I was still living in Hawaii but was spending much time in the Bay Area. As the option date drew nigh, it became apparent that I would have to move here. My father never pushed me to do that—he left it up to me to make what he knew and I found out was the inevitable decision. My wife, Pat, and I bought a home in Hillsborough in August, commissioned some changes, and moved in with our two young children (Lee and Jack) in November, 1960. I was thirty two years old. My brother, Bob, age 29, with his wife and family moved to Hillsborough as well. Dick, age 25, having finished the El Paso project and moved to Hawaii, remained in Hawaii to finish the Foster Tower Hotel which was under construction. He moved to Hillsborough in 1963 with his family.

The decision was made to close the Oklahoma City home office and move it to California. An office was rented in Burlingame, upstairs in a shopping center in the Mills Estate. There was a restaurant/bar below us which used redwood gutters as part of the decor on the facade. So they named the bistro "The Gutter." In directing people to our office, we had to tell them that we were upstairs over the Gutter. (Later, the landlord secured a name change: at minimum cost the name was changed to "The Putter.") We were to be in that location until our move into our new office building at 1015 East Hillsdale, Foster City, in 1965.

Moving here from Oklahoma City were W. A. "Bill" Innes, a C.P.A. and Dad's right hand man; Ralph Chase, office manager; and Gene Hubbard, accountant. Also moving here was A. O. "Del" Champlin. Del was the senior partner in one of Oklahoma City's better known independent accounting firms. He had provided tax advice and auditing services to the family business for several years and he wanted to be a part of the Foster City venture as he built an accounting business in California. Del's partner,

Kenneth Moak, remained in Oklahoma City and with frequent visits from Oklahoma City remained our auditor even after Del's withdrawal from the firm.

James Aston, president of the Republic National Bank of Dallas, had been a city manager in Texas and was personally acquainted with George Shannon, city manager of Anchorage, Alaska. He knew that George was planning to leave that job after a successful seven years when he earned for the city a *Look Magazine* All America Cities Award, a highly regarded award much sought after by cities all over the country. Aston thought that Shannon would be a good choice for manager of the Estero District. We asked him to come for an interview. He did, and was hired without our considering any other candidate. He proved to be a great choice and gave exceptional service to the development.

CHAPTER THREE

Design

WILSEY & HAM, known as Wilsey Ham & Blair in the 60's, was located in Millbrae and enjoyed an outstanding reputation as civil engineers, land planners and architects. With a state wide reputation, they were especially well regarded in San Mateo County where they had deep roots. The founder, Earl P. Wilsey, having retired from the firm, was a former city manager of Hillsborough. Lee Ham, the young senior partner and CEO, was a long time County resident with a long record of service to his community. The firm had done all of Dick Grant's work. He and others with whom we had checked considered them first rate and of the highest integrity. We looked no further and brought them into the process at the outset, while basic feasibility was being considered. They were to do both the civil engineering and the general plan with the specific plans that would follow.

They had done some large developments but this job was a dream. They performed extremely well. Lee Ham never allowed his enthusiasm for the job to cloud his advice in any way that might lure us into avenues we should not go. His advice and counsel accompanying his professional work was valuable and always reliable.

He assembled a first rate planning department. Gordon Tillson was supervising partner, George S. Gatter was project manager, and Abraam Krushkhov, a partner in the land planning firm of Ruth + Krushkhov, was brought in to take the lead in Foster City's design. Michael McDougall was a principal planner and played a major role. Mike went on to become a professor of land planning at California Polytechnic University, San Luis Obispo, and he would bring his class to Foster City from time to time to view the truly planned community he helped to create.

Some of the guidelines which the planners were to use:

i.   Industrial park located north of the master planned Highway 92. That area was a fairly ideal size for the industrial base that we committed to develop as part of the balanced tax base that we sought for the total development.

ii. Placement of the lagoon to secure the best drainage of the land with the least amount of fill.

iii. A system of arterial streets to allow easy vehicular access to the farthest reaches of Foster City.

iv. Residential neighborhoods of a size to accommodate an elementary school. The boundaries of each neighborhood would be the lagoon or an arterial street.

v.   A central shopping area plus neighborhood convenience shopping areas. The neighborhood centers were to be on the lagoon to allow shopping by water access.

This preliminary plan was entitled *"Brewer Island today—Foster City tomorrow."* It was dated July, 1960, one month before we exercised the option to buy the land. It seemed to meet most of the criteria. My father was concerned however that the main retail commercial land was not well located. It fronted the town center lake on its east side, somewhat near where the Walker Recreation Building is today, and was about a half mile off of Highway 92. He wondered if the number of neighborhood shopping centers was right, so he called in a consultant, Larry Smith & Associates, of Seattle, who had a national reputation for shopping center economics.

After studying the plan, Larry Smith & Associates concluded that it was unlikely that a commercially successful shopping center could be built at the indicated location. First and foremost, for any hope of success it had to have easy access to Highway 92. Second, the orientation on the lake, while attractive, created design problems from a commercial point of view. And finally, Hillsdale Shopping Center, one mile from Foster City on Hillsdale Blvd., was extreme competition and under the best of conditions, the Foster City commercial center would be hard pressed to compete. Even if it could count on all of the business from Foster City residents, which it could not, it would have to be good enough to pull trade from surrounding areas.

Dad ordered the general plan to be revised, with the central business area placed next to the freeway (where the Town Center is today) as the Larry

Smith firm suggested. There were to be three neighborhood convenience centers, all located on the lagoon, plus another small one near the eastern edge of the island, on the Bay. It was felt that the convenience centers on the lagoon could be designed in a manner that would allow shopping by boat, which set them apart from the ordinary neighborhood center.

A major consideration in the development of the general plan was the total ultimate value of the land and buildings which would follow. The planners and engineers, working together, stayed aware of the total costs of the development and the need for land use intensive enough to have a value which would pay the costs. With the anticipated Estero Municipal Improvement District and the general obligation bonds that would be issued for the development, it was essential that the values being created would provide the necessary taxes at affordable rates. Foster City could not afford low density land uses like golf courses and big residential lots. While the assessed valuation behind the Estero District was the primary concern, there was also concern that Foster City not be a tax drain on the school districts in which it was located.

Market considerations could not be ignored. We knew that the single family home market was extremely good in San Mateo County. This use of the land consumed land at the fastest rate, so it was essential that it be developed first and at a rapid rate. Clearly, the commercial development could not occur until there was a population in Foster City. It was believed that apartment development would be successful at an early date.

Our market research told us that the industrial land would be slow. Both South San Francisco and Burlingame/Millbrae (Mills Estate) had land for sale that was better located at the time than was Foster City. Closeness to San Francisco and San Francisco International Airport gave those areas the edge. No one would have predicted that the Foster City industrial land would eventually become highly marketable as a result of high tech industrial growth from the south, namely Silicon Valley.

The single family lot, being our most important product, had to be carefully designed. How big should the typical lot be? 55' x 100'? 60' x 100'? 65' x 100'? The standard finally adopted was 65' x 95'. The curvature of the shoreline determined by the layout of the lagoon dictated that the streets would be curvilinear. This was felt to provide the most attractive and interesting streets. The curving streets and numerous cul de sacs would produce lots larger than the conventional rectangle.

Lots located on the shore of the lagoon would be the most valuable, so consideration was given to how to maximize this type of land. This was done by the creation of the islands. With a lagoon of four miles in length, the addition of islands enabled us to have thirteen miles of shoreline.

The Foster City islands are connected by a strip of land. Rather than making the "strip" wide enough to have lots fronting the street, we chose to keep it narrow with views of the lagoon on both sides. The goal was that this entrance to the island be like a bridge. A culvert had to be put under that strip to avoid trapping stagnant water in the lagoon. We added several feet of fill to the strip, creating a hill of sorts, in order to enhance the bridge feeling. Benches were installed at the peak of the "bridge" to allow viewing down the strip of water leading to the bigger lagoon. With just a single "bridge" to each island, the entire waterfront on both sides of what has become known as the "narrow water" was accessible for boating. The islands were made parallel to the main shore line, versus creating fingers perpendicular to the shore, to encourage the most effective flushing of the lagoon, without trapping water.

To protect and stabilize the banks or shoreline of the lagoon, it was decided that the narrow waterways would be lined with concrete walls. The retaining wall is an inverted T with half of the cross bar of the T covered with earth and the other half on the floor of the lagoon. The wall is five feet high.

For the wider waterways, it was decided to leave it a sloping bank covered with rip-rap, consisting of large gravel. This allowed the owner to maintain it as is or rebuild it in some fashion. Later, in the 1970's, after incorporation, the City decided that all waterfront properties which had not been built upon should have to install a wall or bulkhead of the City's choosing. The City chose a system made from aluminum. To get a building permit on the lot, you had to have complied. Thirty years later, there developed evidence of widespread failure of the aluminum walls, whereas the old concrete walls are doing fine and the slopes still stand on many lots or have been replaced by some other system.

Partners of T. Jack Foster & Sons surround a model of Foster City.
From the left: T. Jack Foster, John R. (Bob) Foster,
Richard H. (Dick) Foster, and T. Jack Foster, Jr.

The lagoon areas were deeded to the Estero District (EMID) for the storage and flow of water, reserving an easement for boating and recreational use for the benefit of all the property owners in Foster City; it was subject only to rules and regulations to be promulgated for the benefit of all. Not given to EMID was the lagoon area extending fifteen feet from the land. Instead, an easement for the storage and flow of water was given, but we reserved the ownership of the submerged land for the adjacent owner so that they could build their boat docks on their own property.

The earliest thinking envisioned a marina on Belmont Slough. the waterway that marked Foster City's southern boundary and separated it from what became Redwood Shores. The July 1960 plan, *"Brewer Island today—Foster City tomorrow,"* showed a marina or yacht club with dockage in the Bay and also in the lagoon. We thought that there might be demand for transfer of boats from one body of water to the other, and consideration was given to building a lock for that purpose.

Early on, the decision was made to allow only non-power boats in the lagoon; it was felt that the noise, and the waves created by their wakes would be objectionable. It would be better to make that decision at the outset rather than to try to implement it later, after the power boat advocates were established. Electric boats were excluded from the ban, as they are quiet and slow. As we began to focus on the nature of the boating in the lagoon, the lock system was abandoned, feeling that whatever need there was to move boats from one marina to the other could be done by some system of cranes.

Eventually, it was concluded that a marina on the Bay could not be this far up Belmont Slough, and should be "down water," closer to the Bay. Moreover, if Foster City Blvd. were ever to be extended to connect to Redwood Shores, the marina should be below it, toward the east. The City of Foster City continued to pursue a marina in this location into the mid-1980's when it considered a joint venture with the then-owner of the land.

This July 1960 plan did not show a connection to Redwood Shores but did show a direct connection of a major arterial street from the Ralston/101 interchange, crossing Foster City in a big loop extending almost to the east shore, crossing Highway 92 and connecting to the end of Third Avenue. It also appeared on a map in an EMID Bond prospectus in 1964.

That Foster City would have a connection to the land to the south, whenever it developed, was never in doubt and Foster City Blvd. seemed the logical place. In time, as the later neighborhoods were designed, an alternate and better connection was envisioned at the end of Edgewater Blvd. in Neighborhood 8. As that street narrows, adequate right of way was preserved on both sides to allow future widening. Also, where the street ends, at Baffin, a right of way exists to allow extension of Edgewater Blvd. across what appears to be parkland. It aligns perfectly with Island Drive in Redwood Shores, so perfectly that it suggests that the planners there also anticipated a connection.

Frankly, while I know it would be a political hot potato, I earnestly believe that such a connection would be in the best interests of almost everybody, especially the residents of Foster City, commuting south. They now must drive north to Hillsdale Blvd. to get to Bayshore to then drive south. I think that it could save up to three miles on the commute for some. The relief on Bayshore would be so significant that the State Highway Department should insist upon it.

We badly wanted to do something about the parade of electrical transmission lines crossing Foster City. Pacific Gas & Electric Co. (P.G.&E) offered no help, as we investigated placing the lines underground. That proved impossible so we considered rerouting them around Foster City, offshore, on the Bay side. The State master plan called for the Bay Front Freeway to be built from San Jose to San Francisco, in the Bay, on a combination of fill and causeways or bridges. It seemed logical to put the transmission towers in that location, between Foster City's eastern shore and the freeway. The cost estimate was $11 million. Even if we could have managed that, P.G.&E. said it wouldn't work. Sometimes things just have a way of working out. The freeway got cancelled, the transmission towers stayed where they were, and Foster City is better for it.

The question of putting the electrical and telephone distribution underground though was never in doubt. P.G.&E. at first said that it was not acceptable, that such a large system had never been built under ground. We said that it had to be done. We hired an electrical engineer, Kenward S.

Oliphant, to figure out how to do it. He presented a solution to P.G.&E. and they accepted it. Oliphant designed the entire underground distribution system for Foster City. It turned out that the transformer boxes had to be above ground, but we eliminated the most objectionable: the power poles and overhead wires.

They are objectionable, aesthetically, anywhere, but nowhere more than in an area like Foster City. The density and flatness of Foster City would have produced thousands of poles and a network of overhead wires. Some communities try to deal with this problem by putting the system on the rear lot lines where they are less obvious. With thirteen miles of lagoon shoreline in Foster City, where do the poles go? On the waterfront or the street? The Oliphant design became the standard used by P.G.&E. throughout their system.

Another great efficiency and economy evolved when Oliphant, with Wilsey & Ham's cooperation and blessing, coordinated the undergrounding for all the utilities: primary and secondary electric, street lighting, police and fire signals, telephone, gas, water, sewer and storm drain. In order to minimize the depth and number of trenches, he determined the order of utilities to go into each trench. Further coordination was needed with sidewalks, curbs, catch basins, paving, bridges, driveways, transformer pads, and so on. Then coordination was with the different contractors who were instructed as to when it was their turn to install the particular utility for which they were responsible. Oliphant describes the complexity and the savings in an article which he wrote for the March 1966 issue of *Electrical Construction and Maintenance*, a McGraw-Hill publication. Kenward S. Oliphant's contribution to Foster City was innovative and very significant

"Brewer Island today—Foster City tomorrow," the July 1960 plan document, incorporated the criteria which the San Mateo school district wanted to be used for future schools in Foster City. The enrollment was calculated to be from 500 to 1000 at each school which required 10 acres for 500 pupils and 15 acres for 1000. The planners split the difference and planned that each school have 800 students on 13 acres. This resulted in the projected need for 8 or 9 elementary schools, each on 13 acres plus two junior high (middle) schools of 20 acres. There was to be a junior high school on the east side and one on the west.

The planners translated this criteria into numbers of families, and homes that were appropriate for each school. This determined the size of the nine neighborhoods. To quote from *"Brewer Island today—Foster City tomorrow,"*:

All elementary schools will be at the center of neighborhoods. With arterial streets generally bounding neighborhoods, and with moderately higher population density, all youngsters will be within 2000 feet of their school and neighborhood playground and may reach them without crossing major traffic thereby eliminating need for an expensive bus system.

In time, the school district decided that it wanted fewer and larger schools and only one junior high school. Thus, the schools are only in Neighborhoods 1, 2 and 9 with the planned school sites in 4 and 8 converted to other uses. The site in number 3, adjacent to the junior high school site was sold off by the district for housing development. The rest of the neighborhoods had not yet been planned, so the school sites were left out, including the junior high school site. The most basic determinant of a neighborhood size then became irrelevant.

The high school superintendent, Tom Reynolds, said he wanted two high school sites, each about forty acres. He was the great builder of high schools with Hillsdale, Aragon, Mills and Capuchino to his credit. The planners said that there was no way that Foster City could justify two high school sites and urged me to resist Mr. Reynolds. I told him that we had no intention of including two high school sites in our general plan. We wanted only one high school so it could occupy a prominent place in the town center area. He finally relented, but I never understood why he wanted a second site unless it was for another high school in the eastern part of San Mateo.

The planners put the high school in the center of town, south of civic center and across the street from Central Park. The site was 40 acres plus 16 under the transmission lines. This area could be used for parking, open space and certain sports activities. In keeping with our policy of selling land to public entities at our cost, the San Mateo High School paid $800,000 for this land being 40 acres at $20,000 per acre and the 16 encumbered acres being a gift.

Later school boards decided that, with the number of high schools that it already had in the district, though poorly located in terms of distribution, a new high school in Foster City could not be justified and proceeded to divest itself of the 56 acre site, making Foster City the largest city in California without a high school. As this started to happen in the 1980's, it was recognized the harm that would be done to the Foster City plan, so under the leadership of Assemblyman Robert Naylor, a law was passed which effectively required the district to donate half of the land to Foster City. The district sold the southern half, taking $10 million profit which was put into existing schools. The city of Foster City came into ownership of the remaining acres adjacent to Civic Center.

The planners needed direction to accommodate the church needs of the community. I contacted the Northern California Council of Churches which led to a meeting with Bishop Richard Millard, of the Episcopal Dioceses of San Francisco. From that time on, he was the man who helped develop the church master plan for Foster City. The planners suggested that, citywide, forty acres be devoted to churches. We concluded that the sites should range somewhat in size from two acres up to six acres, the larger sites being able to accommodate schools. There would be two large sites, with one for the Catholic Church. An effort would be made to divide the other sites to best serve the entire community. We charged $20,000 per acre, the same as for school sites. We reserved the right to buy it back at that price to prevent land speculation and to make more certain that a church would be built.

One of our goals for Foster City was to create a "sense of place." This is a feeling that, wherever you are in Foster City, you know you are in Foster City. Our neighboring Peninsula communities which had evolved slowly over a hundred plus years until they grew right up to each other, have no such identity. Certainly the downtowns might have their own personalities, but in the neighborhoods one can be totally confused as to which town they are in.

Some of the ways that we hoped to give that "sense of place" to Foster City were frequent views of the lagoon, an occasional high rise building in view to allow orientation, lack of overhead wires with attendant poles, spacious arterial streets, and a family of street "furniture" that was attractive and unique to Foster City.

T. JACK FOSTER, JR.

To help create that design look, we hired James K. Levorsen, AIA. He was our architectural consultant for street furniture plus other matters needing design help.

The street lights are an example of such street furniture. Oliphant designed the street light system for Foster City, but Levorsen consulted on what the light standards would look like. In the residential areas, we all agreed that the standards should be low in scale to go with the homes. Levorsen came up with a design of a light fixture with fins around it. The vertical fins could be placed close together or far apart as needed to throw the light where it was wanted (on the streets and sidewalks) and to shield it from shining where it was not wanted (on the houses). Painted beige as were the poles, they glowed attractively at night as they lined the residential streets. The fins had the additional advantage of protecting the lens from vandals and the wind. In later years, after incorporation, the City availed itself of the newest street lighting technology and replaced all these residential standards. The new lights were more economical and efficient to operate. In the book, *A New Town Comes of Age: Foster City, California,* a picture of the old standard can be found on page 85. I recall several chilly evenings when we all gathered in Foster City to look at the sample light as the design was evolving. The viewers included, among others, Levorsen, Oliphant, Estero District officials George Shannon and Jack Davis, County Engineer Don Wilson, and myself.

The arterial lights were not custom designed, but selected from the good designs then available. With Levorsen's advice we added a shield around the light and painted the whole standard blue. The shields have since been removed, but the color blue remains.

The major supplier of fireplugs to cities and developments was Greenberg and Sons of San Francisco. Manufacturing as they did in San Francisco, they had the fire plug market for Northern California virtually tied up. Without shopping around, we asked them if they would consider designing a new look in fire plugs. They said yes, and asked us what we had in mind.

I said, "How about a plug that you could sit down on?"

They said that they would try.

Again, with Levorsen consulting, the first new design in fire plugs in many years evolved. The first prototype was shown to us with the valves on the top — for ease of the firemen using their wrenches to open the valve.

I said, "You can't sit on that."

The final design had the valves in back and it won a national design award. I still get a kick out of seeing someone in Foster City sitting on a fire plug. We were told that functionally this design outperformed the old plugs in that there is less turbulence from the water pressure. Greenberg now sells this plug extensively.

In the unincorporated areas of the County, the standard color for street name signs was green but for Foster City, we wanted to use blue in keeping with our water oriented theme. We asked Don Wilson, County Engineer, permission to deviate from the County standard and install blue signs. I think he was beginning to tire of acceding to our requests to be different, so he said "no," so green it was. I was pleased to see that the City, in later years when it came time to change what had become the "old" signs, changed them to blue. It is a coincidence that the City chose the color that we wanted to use in the first place.

In Neighborhood #1, there are lots backing up to Hillsdale Blvd. and a wall was needed to screen the back yards from the boulevard. Levorsen designed a row of reinforced concrete vertical slabs as the wall. Since there might be differential settlement along such a long length of wall, he staggered the placement of the slabs to allow a space between. By making them different heights, any settlement along the way would not show. They still stand and have been restored and painted by the City with new landscaping between the wall and the sidewalk.

T. JACK FOSTER, JR.

CHAPTER FOUR

The Fill

FROM THE BEGINNING it was known that an enormous amount of fill would be required to raise the level of Foster City for drainage purposes. Another need for fill stemmed from the nature of the soil that was there. Being bay mud over 60 feet deep, though dry on the surface, it had no structural quality. While the civil engineers (Wilsey, Ham & Blair) wanted fill for drainage, the soils engineers (Dames & Moore) wanted it for strength.

One doesn't think about soil as being "strong" but in the world of soils engineering, it is very important. Soil must be strong enough to support the structures that you may want to build. Solid rock is the best. If it is not rock, but gravel or sand or dirt, it must be capable of being compacted, that is, pressed together so as to make it like rock, with the moisture squeezed out. Bay mud, even if dried out so that it becomes dirt, is impossible to compact. If water is added, it becomes bay mud again whereas a proper fill, properly compacted, is undisturbed by moisture.

It was impossible to compact the 60 feet deep bay mud. The answer was to place a layer of compacted fill on top of the existing bay mud. Even then, care had to be given to the weight of the structure placed on top. For example, a multistory building would clearly be too heavy. Its weight would be felt beyond the fill and would begin to sink. The answer in that case would be to use piles. These are posts driven deep into the ground and the building placed on the posts. In some situations, piles are driven until they reach solid rock. In Foster City, however, they use "friction" piles which, at some depth are held in place by the pressure on the sides of the pile. The type of pile and its length depends on the weight of the building.

The use of piles opens the door to other problems which the engineers have to solve. They know that the piles will carry the entire weight of the building, whereas the area surrounding the building will settle over time with the rest of the land around it. The land will settle away from the building. Sidewalks won't line up with the entrances. The pipelines into the building will break. These problems, when understood, are accommodated in the design.

In another example, in Foster City, the bridges are on piles. The street pavement onto the bridge consists of a long slab of reinforced concrete with one end supported by the piles and the other end on grade As the land settles, the road remains connected to the bridge. There are many pile supported structures in Foster City—all successful.

The original Wells Fargo Building, located at Hillsdale Blvd. and across Shell Blvd. from the present branch, posed an interesting design problem. Though a small two story building, it was required to have a vault. The vault would weigh much heavier than the rest of the building, and would cause the building to settle unevenly and toward the corner of the building where the vault was located. The engineers preferred to avoid the use of piles for various reasons, including cost. Their solution was to excavate the earth including the compacted fill, beneath the vault only. This would lighten the combined weight of fill and building at that part of the building, to make it equal to the combined weight of fill and building of the rest of the building. Their solution worked perfectly.

The issue at the outset was how much fill for proper drainage and how high should it be. Wilsey & Ham presented two different concepts: 1. raise the island enough for storm water to drain directly into the Bay and, 2. create a lagoon system to collect the storm water which could be pumped from the island, and raise the balance of the land high enough for the storm water to drain to the lagoon. Like a saucer, the rain that fell on the island would have to be captured in the lagoons and then pumped off. The second system amounted to an average fill depth of six feet. Dames & Moore allowed that as long as the fill was of a certain structural quality and compacted, that depth would be adequate.

County Engineer Don Wilson, afraid to rely on pumps for drainage and flood control advocated plan #1. The engineers had calculated that plan #1 would require 45 million cubic yards of fill while plan #2 needed 18 million cubic yards. With plan #1 the fill at the center of the island would be over fifty feet high. Aside from the economics of such a fill, which would doom the project, the practical feasibility was equally impossible. Dames & Moore advised that such a depth of fill was impossible to achieve as the weight would cause the fill to simply sink into the mud, pushing out or up at some unknown point.

Even the weight of the 18 million yards had to be dealt with. The calculation was made that the level of the city would sink, overall, by as much as two feet, the first one foot as soon as the fill was placed on it and the second foot over a period of years. This factor influenced the engineering design that followed. Streets had to drain after settlement and pipelines that depended on gravity, versus pumps, had to continue to flow in the same design direction.

As the underlying mud gets slightly compacted by the weight of the fill, the engineers must remain mindful that the mud has a tendency to want to push back up if it can find a place of weakness. The engineers cautioned that the weight of the water in the lagoon is important in holding the mud in its place. If the lagoons were drained for some reason, there is danger that the mud in the channels could rise and the higher adjacent land could sink!

Recognizing that basic feasibility hung in the balance, the Board of Supervisors, satisfied with the quality of engineering being presented by the two firms, voted unanimously to accept the saucer concept—plan #2. Engineer Wilson graciously accepted the decision of the Board, and continued to work with and cooperate with the developers in the ongoing development.

Consideration also had to be given to the type of fill. Was it to be dry fill, excavated from a mountain someplace, or wet fill, dredged onto the land? Wet fill is fill from under the Bay, capable of being transported by water. The belief was that wet fill would be cheaper and the filling operation would be less disruptive of the region. The first effort was a negotiation with Utah Construction Company, the large San Francisco company which owned some large dredges and had a record of successful completion of dredged fill operations, such as Alameda in the East Bay.

One problem was that there was no suitable material for fill in the Bay close to the island. The mud offshore had no structural quality and could not be used. The nearest was a sand deposit offshore of the San Francisco airport, which was owned by the State of California. There is no better fill than sand as it compacts easily and, when compacted, is structurally sound. This deposit was called San Bruno Shoals. We found that Estero Municipal Improvement District (more later) could lease this deposit with an agreement that paid a royalty to the State of 10 cents per cubic yard. The State got the added benefit of enlarging the Bay with the excavation.

This sand deposit was five miles from Brewer Island. Utah Construction Co. figured the job, including pumping the sand the entire five mile distance, plus the additional distance for it to reach across the island. Brewer Island is about two miles across. This is not an impossible task in the dredging business, but it proved to be much too expensive.

A dry fill solution was sought. The source that might be feasible was San Bruno Mountain, which was owned by the Crocker Land Company. Bill Morton was the manager of the company and he and his staff expressed a willingness to consider a plan to allow the removal of 18 million yards of earth from that source. The engineers went to work to devise a plan. Morton's requirement, appropriately, was that the earth be removed in such a fashion that would terrace and shape the mountain so that it could be developed into residential lots. The engineers designed a system of grading and excavation including enclosed conveyer belt that would have taken the rock to hoppers where large earth moving trucks could be filled and dispatched down Bayshore Highway to the future Foster City. A cost figure was determined.

In another meeting with Morton, the costs were revealed together with the value to the Crocker land. If Crocker would pay a part of the costs, Foster City could afford the balance and both lands would be graded, ready for development. Morton responded that Crocker would pay none of the cost but would allow the fill to be removed with appropriate protections and guaranties. Once again, it was too expensive for just Foster City to bear. As I drive along the Bayshore, past San Bruno Mountain, I often reflect on the business opportunity missed by the Crocker Land Company in refusing to pay any of the cost of grading their mountain.

Later, the Crocker Land Company entered a joint venture agreement with Ideal Cement Company, which owned the submerged land offshore of Foster City, and Rockefeller Bros. of New York and Lazard Freres of Paris and New York. The plan was to fill the Ideal property with the rock from

San Bruno Mountain, financed by the New York interests. The formation of the Bay Conservation and Development Commission ended that plan, forever. Later Crocker made still another effort to develop the land, this time without the Bay fill aspect, in a joint venture with American Factors of Honolulu and W. W. Dean, local home builder and developer. The Mission Blue butterfly was discovered on the slopes of the mountain, and development efforts were again halted.

As we began to despair over finding an economical solution, we were approached by a small dredging company named Associated Dredging Company. They had a plan to use a small dredge to excavate the sand from San Bruno Shoals and put it into a barge which would then be brought to the edge of the island. The sand would be dumped under water, and then redredged onto the land, with a small dredge. This multiple handling of the fill seemed illogical, but with the ability to use small dredges pumping shorter distances, it made sense. Furthermore, the dredges were available as were two earth moving barges, with gates that allowed the release of sand into the water. The only problem was, the barges were in Utah; they had been specially built for a large fill project in the Great Salt Lake.

The decision was made to go forward with this plan. The mineral lease on San Bruno Shoals was secured from the State. One problem was that Associated Dredging Company was small, and short on financing capacity. The Estero Municipal Improvement District was leery of awarding such a large contract to such a small company. Finally, with the approval of the lawyers including those representing the bond consultants, my father formed a dredging company and subcontracted the work to Associated Dredging Company. With his personal guarantee, he effectively removed the concern the lawyers had about awarding the contract. We were all aware of the potential conflict of interest, either real or perceived, so the contract was written to alleviate concerns that some might have regarding my father dealing with the District in this manner. There was no profit in the contract and the relationship, examined numerous times, including by the Attorney General of the State, was not criticized. Eventually, after operating for enough time for all to be comfortable, the bond council of the Estero District suggested that the arrangement be ended. The District now contracted directly with Associated and my father withdrew, happily and without profit or loss. His association with the operation had served its purpose.

An aerial view of Foster City in August 1962. Dredged fill is being placed in Neighborhood 1 and the excavation for the lagoon has commenced.

The mobilization for the fill operation began. The Estero District had negotiated for the purchase of the two barges. They were huge, big enough to carry 2,000 cubic yards of sand. That is equal to 120 double gondola truck loads. A contract was awarded for the dismantling of the barges in Utah, their shipment to the Bay Area, and the reassembly. With cutting torches and cranes, the two barges were cut into as many parts as could be loaded onto 86 freight cars. They were brought by Southern Pacific to a shipyard in the East Bay where they were unloaded and reassembled.

After putting them back together, they were christened by my Mother, invited by the shipyard. She smashed the bottle of champaign onto the bow as the barge slid into the water. The second barge was launched with similar ceremony. In the reassembly there was a redesign to lower the superstructure of the barges. If this were not done, when returning empty at maximum height above the water and at high tide, the topmost part would not clear the old San Mateo-Hayward bridge, necessitating raising the lift section of the bridge several times a day. This was not good for operations, needless to say the public relations with the Highway 92 motorists.

Preparation of the rehandling area, the place where the barges would dump the sand to be then dredged onto the land, consisted of creating a channel from the shipping channel to the shoreline of Foster City near the present end of Tarpon Street adjacent to the levee. Then, a basin was dredged. A large wooden dry dock, acquired in the east Bay, was brought to the site and lowered into the basin. It was originally built for the purpose of raising boats out of the water, but here it was to remain submerged and become the underwater hopper to receive the fill. Pusher type tug boats maneuvered the large barges over the dry dock/hopper where the bottom gates of the barge were opened and the sand was allowed to fall out. It took two hours to load a barge, and one minute to empty it.

There were pipes with openings affixed to the bottom of the dry dock/hopper, which were attached to a dredge line. A pump sucked the sand and transported it by water through lengthy pipelines onto the land. The pipeline over the land extended a distance of two miles at times. Eventually, the operator was to abandon the fixed pipes on the bottom of the hopper and replace it with a movable dredge on the surface.

Preparation on the land to receive the dredged fill consisted of a series of temporary retaining levees, confining areas that tapered to a single point for each group of areas, where the water was drained off. It was like pieces of a pie, all tapering to the same point: each section, or "piece," was filled, starting at the wide part and moving to the point. As the area filled, a tractor ran back and forth over the new fill squeezing the water out. The water then went to the point where a pump got rid of it. Then the fill started at the next section without the need to move the water disposing pump. Squeezing the water out is how sand is compacted.

The dredge water still had very fine sand in it Because this very fine material had little structural strength, an area had to be found to accommodate it, one that would not be needed for many years. It was pumped to a holding area to allow the grains to sink. The then clear water was pumped into the Bay. The area chosen was the acreage north of Third Ave., where the golf facility is currently located. This had been a very shallow area of about 123 acres which we owned and saw very little use for. Levees were created by excavation from the Bay, and the newly created land eventually became available for limited use.

Other land preparation matters concerned the excavation for the lagoon. The engineers had decided that 460 acre feet of emergency storm water storage was needed for Foster City drainage purposes. Normally, the pumps could be expected to expel storm water at the rate it was raining, but in the event of a very heavy rain or a breakdown of the pumps, emergency storage was required. (The pumps are diesel operated and not dependent on electricity.)

The required 460 acre feet is defined by engineers as a measure of capacity for water equal in size to 460 acres at one foot in depth. This capacity can be provided in a basin 6 feet deep by 77 acres, or 5 feet deep by 92 acres. The decision was made to create for Foster City a lagoon system of 230 acres with the top two feet serving the emergency function. In the summer the lagoon is allowed to fill for recreation and aesthetic purposes. In the winter, when rain is expected, the lagoon level is lowered by two feet to provide that emergency storage capacity. The City has complete control of the water level by opening gates at the south end and allowing the Bay water to enter and removing water at the north end with the pumps. It sometimes uses this feature to simply circulate the lagoon water.

The excavation of the lagoon started almost immediately. The earliest pictures of the land area of Foster City shows the beginning of that excavation near Shooting Star Isle. The lagoon excavation proceeded so rapidly that in a regular weekly meeting of the engineers, the planners, the Estero District, and ourselves, one of the planners mentioned that they wanted to make a slight change in the location of a part of the lagoon. The engineer said, "Too late. It's already been dug." There is a "notch" in the shoreline, near the northern end of the Shell Blvd. bridge that resulted from the failed effort by the planners to realign the lagoon.

Other land preparations included the removal of the top few inches of soil from the island and stockpiling it for use later as top-soil, primarily in the parks, but also in other areas where top-soil was needed. The main reason was the soils engineers did not want that soil underneath the compacted sand as it had old vegetation in it.

About one third of the island was in salt ponds. Dames & Moore required that we drain them and allow them to dry out for some years before the land could be filled.

The material excavated to create the lagoons could not be used as structural fill, so uses for that soil had to be found. In some cases, it was put in the lower areas of the island where the old sloughs used to be, then the compacted sand fill was put over it. However, we still could not build on that area of the old sloughs and had to put about four or five feet of additional fill on top of the lot for a few years, eventually to remove it for use. The weight of this "surcharge" material, as we called it, compressed the soil beneath to make it more equal to the surrounding ground. Even then, extra reinforcing was required for the concrete in the foundations of the houses on those lots, extra above the special foundations required on "normal" Foster City lots. These were all requirements of Dames & Moore and were reviewed and approved by the Federal Housing Administration. No lot was ever released for construction without a certification by Dames & Moore.

The care given to the design and placement of the fill was to ensure that the settlement that was expected (about two feet over time) would be substantially equal.. Because the fill was compacted when it was placed on the surface, the future settlement was of the mud and was a result of the weight of the compacted fill. The buildings added weight as well, but not nearly as much as the fill. We did not want any buildings to tilt or break as a result of excessive differential settlement, defined as two areas close by each other which settle differently. Foundations were designed to be continuous and strong to accommodate slight differential settlement. Excessive differential settlement over a broader area could also cause sewer and storm drain lines to reverse their flow.

The other consideration was earthquake. The shock waves from an earthquake were expected to travel through the mud with the result that the initial shock would be dampened but the amplification would be increased. It is this shaking that causes so much damage. The engineer who explained this to me said, "Think of Jello." The compacted fill on the top would help to decrease this impact and the reinforced foundations would help to "ride out" the quake without damage. Flexibility built into the utility lines would allow movement of the lines without damage.

The soils engineers were confident that liquefaction would not be a problem. Liquefaction is a phenomenon when loose wet sand is shaken by an earthquake in such a way that the sand sinks and the water comes to the top. The result is a piece of ground that appears damp, becomes a pool of water with an earthquake. The only sand in Foster City is the imported fill and the water was forced out of it as it was compacted. At the outset, prior to the placement of any fill, cores were drilled all over Foster City to determine what was underneath. There was no sand at any layer so no evidence that liquefaction had ever occurred before. With no sand, liquefaction would not have been possible. With compacted sand, it is not possible either.

In marketing Foster City, putting the earthquake situation into perspective was always a problem. It was not a great sales point to advertise that the land had been prepared in such a way that earthquakes would not be as damaging as they would otherwise be. It was dealt with to some extent in the official subdivision report that is required by the Department of Real Estate to be furnished to all buyers. The biggest problem came from the U. S. Geological Survey which released a report to the press from time to time stating that the greatest damage from an earthquake would be along the filled areas at the edge of the Bay. Their report always included a map, in case there was any doubt about where the shores of the Bay were but their report always ignored the fact that Foster City was covered with compacted fill. On the map, it looked just as bad as the rest of the bad areas. They even had a map showing the areas around the Bay that could have liquefaction. On the Foster City map, they showed such spots scattered here and there, as if there was a difference. There clearly was no difference. If one part of Foster City was susceptible to liquefaction, it all was.

Whenever the USGS reports hit the newspapers as they did with some regularity, sales in Foster City seemed to slow down or stop for a time. I would call Bill Moore of Dames & Moore and ask, "Bill, this publicity is killing us. What can we do about it?" He would reply, "Jack, we can do nothing. We will be vindicated when we have an earthquake."

I had to wait until October, 1989, when the Bay Area was hit by the Loma Prieta quake. With some glee, I called Bill and said: "Bill, you were right. All the papers reporting on quake damage in the area specifically mention Foster City as being damage free."

My wife and I, with some friends, had left home the day before the earthquake for Manaus, Brazil, where we boarded a ship for a trip up the Amazon. Another passenger on the ship was a guest lecturer who worked at the USGS in Menlo Park. When we met, he recognized my connection with Foster City. When I found out what he did, I told him that his employer was responsible for one of my major recurring nightmares back in the 1960's.

Some of our traveling companions had brought short-wave radios for the purpose of picking up the world series games at Candlestick Park between the Giants and the A's. That is how we learned about the quake. When I finally got my turn at the shortwave radio on the ship in order to call home for a report on the damage, I learned that Foster City was damage free. I could hardly wait to see my new acquaintance from USGS to tell him that Foster City came through the quake just fine. He paused and then he said, "Damn!" (I don't think he really meant it.)

The earthquake question came up so frequently that we did finally publish a brochure attempting to put it in a reasonable perspective. It quotes mainly from the FHA who had studied the matter carefully before accepting Foster City for approval for FHA loans. The director of FHA in San Francisco was willing to be quoted in our brochure.

In June, 1961, standing on the dredge loading sand into barges for fill for Foster City are George Shannon, Manager of Estero Municipal Improvement District, T. Jack Foster, Jr., and T. Jack Foster.

The possibility of a tsunami was also examined. The constricted entrance to the Bay represented by the Golden Gate inlet, limits the power and the range of such a force coming from the Pacific. There have been numerous tsunamis through the years hitting the west coast but none that extended very far into the Bay, certainly not as far south as Foster City. There are no known faults inside the Bay which could otherwise be a problem.

The adequacy of the levees was also examined. This was important to us but also to those agencies and investors who might participate in some way. As we sought to satisfy ourselves on all such matters, we had to be ready to answer questions and share our satisfaction with the results of our investigation, so we sought out the best consultants available.

Dr. Richard Kent, a noted oceanographer and meteorologist was retained for the levee project by Wilsey, Ham & Blair. His study recommended a proper height above sea level for the levees. For the most part, the levees were at that height and very little raising was necessary. The F.H.A. asked the U.S. Army Corps of Engineers for an opinion. and the corps asked for a greater height. Factors influencing the calculation were the maximum lunar tide combined with a storm tide combined with wave run up. Dr. Kent contended that a storm tide required a storm area off shore which would push the tide into the Bay. "Wave run up" is the measure of waves against the levee driven by wind and it requires a storm in the Bay. He calculated that the chances of having both storms so close together at the same time were two in one billion—or some extreme odds like that. The Corps of Engineers was persuaded and Kent's recommendation as to the proper height of levees was accepted.

The engineers examined the strength of the levees and found that they had been well maintained and very little work was needed. With proper maintenance, levees improve with age. The main factor is to check for erosion and to place rip-rap or rock on the outside to prevent wave erosion. A great opportunity came when the old San Mateo Hayward bridge was dismantled and the contractor was seeking a place to put the broken up concrete. We were happy to accept it on the outside of the levees as rip-rap.

The levees on the west side were less important, but still important. They adjoined Marina Lagoon, the waterway owned and operated by the

City of San Mateo as flood protection for the lower areas of San Mateo. Because of some flooding years ago, the City installed tide gates at each end of what was originally called Seal Slough. Storm water draining toward the Bay from much of San Mateo is captured in the lagoon and pumped into the Bay. It has served its purpose well but if there were a failure in the system, the waters would back into San Mateo before the Foster City levees would be topped.

Many years later, in the early 1990's, FEMA advised the City of Foster City that the levee must be raised by 18 inches or flood insurance would be required of all the residents. As other cities and communities in the County have learned, one does not successfully argue with the powerful agency, FEMA. So the City of Foster City spent $2.5 million to raise the levees. The cost was increased by $250,000 when the BCDC required, as a condition of their permit for the fill, the improvement of access over the levee to the Bay for the benefit of the wind surfers. This was a result of the wind surfers' lobby, a powerful group who more recently opposed the expansion of San Francisco airport runways. The windsurfing park off of Third Avenue was the result and continues to be maintained and serviced by the Foster City Parks Department.

Views of Foster City

Photographs by
Jeff Sudmeier and Catherine Miskow

T. JACK FOSTER
FOUNDER OF FOSTER CITY

CHAPTER FIVE

The Bridges

THE FIRST BRIDGE to Foster City was the Twin Bridges over Marina Lagoon, the entrance to Foster City on Hillsdale Blvd. Previously, the only access to Brewer Island was via the two lane (now four) Third Avenue approach road past the garbage dump (now Seal Point Park) to the San Mateo Bridge and was not a satisfactory approach for marketing Foster City. An additional approach had to be found. The only possible access was at Hillsdale, where there was an interchange with Bayshore Highway. The other interchange was at 19th Avenue. but this was destined to become the freeway interchange between highway 101 and the future 92 at some uncertain future date.

My Dad and I called on David Bohannon, the developer of the Hillsdale Shopping Center as well as the rest of the Hillsdale area of San Mateo. He developed many other areas, both in and out of San Mateo County, and was a founder of San Mateo County Development Association, Urban Land Institute, and a past president of the National Association of Home Builders. He received us graciously and was enormously interested in our plans, especially the access via Hillsdale, which at that point was exactly one mile from his regional shopping center. We were certain that he would be anxious that this access be accomplished. He assured us that he would do all that he could to help make it happen including securing the support of the City of San Mateo. My Dad broached that it was going to be necessary to purchase the access, hoping that Bohannon would perhaps assist. He recognized that while it would benefit him, it was a necessity for us. Mr. Bohannon politely declined.

In the course of the conversation, Dad asked if he had ever considered Brewer Island for development purposes. He responded that it had never occurred to him that it was possible for it to be developed.

The point of access at the end of Hillsdale between Norfolk Avenue and Marina Lagoon was vacant. It was owned by the developer of Los

Prados in San Mateo. It was anticipated that some day Hillsdale might be extended to Brewer Island, so this lot was kept vacant and available for that purpose. Unfortunately, the City had not required that it be dedicated as part of the general street dedication of the development, as is usually done, so we had to buy it.

The seller did not hold it for ransom as he might have, but priced it at the market, which seemed high, as the market was determined by what Shell Oil Company had paid for the site next to this one The long range possible extension of Hillsdale eastward onto Brewer Island would make this location a choice corner.

We platted the approach road to the new Twin Bridges through the middle of the site, leaving a landscape area on both sides of the road. Obviously, Shell was disappointed that this plan denied them direct access to Hillsdale. Ultimately, they bought the right of way across the strip to get the direct Hillsdale Boulevard access. This sale helped to recoup some of the cost of the lot.

It was also necessary to secure permission from the City of San Mateo for the bridge, since they owned the lagoon. We got the permit, having negotiated the terms with Mayor Roy Archibald. The terms included the minimum height over the water that the City wanted to accommodate water recreation activities. After the bridge was designed, the contract for construction let, and construction about to begin, Archibald called me and asked if we could make the bridge a little higher. I explained that to do so would cause the design and the budget to be scrapped. A higher bridge is a longer and different bridge, and clearly more costly. He graciously yielded.

I should point out that we entered into these negotiations with the City with some strength behind us. When the Schilling Estate Company previously donated to the City the land that became Marina Lagoon, they reserved the right to cross the lagoon at this point. This right accrued to us when we bought the land. Under that right, we could have done the crossing with a earthen causeway with culverts under it.

The Twin Bridges were designed by George S. Nolte Engineers, San Jose. James Levorsen, AIA, our design consultant advised on the design. Because the approach roads from both sides were divided boulevards, it was decided to create two bridges to respect the joining of the lanes of traffic in each direction and the landscaped space between, the space between the bridges would be a continuation of the median strips.

The design was interesting and unique. The pedestrian walkways were separated from the traffic way by a concrete planter box. Further isolation from the traffic was obtained by lowering the level of the walkway. Attractive decorative lighting was placed in the planter box to light the walkway and to throw limited light onto the traffic ways. A curved planter was placed at the ends of the bridges with a bench.

The traffic engineers obviously felt at that time that two lanes each way represented the proper design for the bridge. The County engineer agreed. It was much later, after Foster City's incorporation, that the new City decided that this was not adequate and rebuilt the bridges to fill in the space between them creating a single bridge with three lanes each way. They replaced the low lights with tall light standards with more light on the pavement. They have maintained the planters, however, and it continues to be a handsome entrance to Foster City.

The next bridge was the "Rainbow Bridge" on Hillsdale Blvd. over the lagoon outlet. This is at the extension of Hillsdale Boulevard which connects Neighborhood #1 with Neighborhood #2. This charming small bridge had the lighting encased in the concrete barrier so to obviate the need for any light poles of any type. Again the pedestrian, protected from traffic by the barrier, walks at a level lower than the traffic way. The bridge rises gently to provide a view over the lake and clearance over the water to allow maintenance craft access to the lagoon from the City's corporation yard on Third Ave.

As with all the Foster City bridges, it meets the goal of being more than just a traffic way across the water. It emphasizes and calls attention to the water, and to itself, as a bridge.

The next bridges, and the most significant ones, were the ones at Foster City Blvd. and Shell Blvd. They were significant because they crossed the Foster City lagoon and were the highest. To allow clearance for the maximum number of types of small sailboats which might be used in Foster City, research told us that 22 feet of clearance was needed. Designed by Wilsey & Ham, the bridges are identical. This saved money not only in design, but also in construction. By scheduling one after the other, rather than simultaneously, one set of concrete forms could be used twice.

Another economy came by making the gradient steeper than normal for high speed bridges. A steeper bridge is a shorter bridge. Aside from the savings, it was felt that aesthetically, the increased gradient provided a bridge-like feel that enhanced the water oriented aspect of Foster City.

The pedestrian walkway was placed through the center of the bridge, with access by walking under the end of the bridge and up a ramp to the walkway, elevated above the traffic way to provide views in all directions. It is a popular place to view the July 4th fireworks show at Central Park. The access beneath the bridge encourages the use of this path for pedestrians to cross the arterial street, not just the lagoon. After the 1989 Loma Prieta earthquake, Foster City embarked on a program of retrofitting much of their public works to the latest earthquake design. These two bridges were not spared. Some beauty was lost, but they are much stronger.

In 1976, when the City built Bi-Centennial Bridge at Beach Park Blvd., the Estero District, therefore the City, still owned the forms used for the Hillsdale and Shell bridges. They could have repeated those economies, but chose to build a totally different, longer bridge with a flatter gradient. It is a beautiful bridge, and maintains the same 22 feet clearance above the water as the other bridges.

CHAPTER SIX

Water and Sewer

THE INITIAL EXPENDITURE and effort to provide water and sewer for a city of 35,000, had to be accomplished before the first house could be occupied.

The Estero District contracted with San Francisco Water Co. for its water supply and the connection was to be made in Hillsborough, at Crystal Springs Road. The pipe line was 24 inches in diameter, steel, cement lined and coated, and capable of carrying 15 million gallons of water a day. The line was installed under Crystal Springs Road through Hillsborough and San Mateo, crossing Marina Lagoon, suspended from the bridge at Third Avenue. It connects with Foster City's two 4 million gallon water tanks on Third Avenue. The tanks were required for emergency purposes. The installation was completed in November, 1962. The tanks were built later.

The 300 acres of Brewers Island which we did not own was in the San Mateo City limits, and was in need of water. In San Mateo, the residents buy their water, not from the city, but from California Water Co. Cal-Water, as it is called, was unable to serve these 300 acres, so the Estero District agreed to serve as the water supplier for this part of San Mateo. An appropriate contract was entered into with the developer. The residents in the Mariner's Island section of San Mateo, pay their water bill to Foster City.

The sewer required a treatment plant with an outfall line which takes the effluent to the deepest part of the bay, which is in the deep water channel under the San Mateo Hayward bridge. The line is a 39 inch steel pipe coated with glass reinforced coal tar enamel and an overcoat of reinforced concrete. It is 6,188 feet long with 3,266 feet extending into the bay. The laying of the part extending into the bay was interesting. First, the trench in the bay was excavated. It is adjacent to the PG&E transmission towers which cross the bay, next to the bridge. The pipeline had been assembled on land on small trolleys, on rail. At the appropriate time, the levee was excavated and the pipe, riding on the trolleys to the water's edge, was pulled out into the bay and positioned over the trench. Then, it was allowed to sink into place. It took less than an hour. This was December, 1962.

CHAPTER SEVEN

The Homes

THE RESIDENTIAL UNITS, particularly the single family houses, were initially the most important item on the agenda. That was the strongest part of the real estate market. Successful development of this part of the plan ensured the success of the rest of the plan.

We started early to find the best of the market builders, good enough and strong enough to compete with each other and to meet the time schedule which we required. They also had to have the strength to meet our terms which called for cash in full when the final map of each subdivision was recorded. The competition with each other was important to us so they would be encouraged to hold their prices down and maximize the value. We wanted a lot of homes built, and built and sold fast, in order to meet our schedule. Our carrot with the builders was that, in order to earn the right to buy lots in additional units, as they became available, they had to "keep up."

To explain the subdivision process, each neighborhood is precisely designed pursuant to the County approved master plan for Foster City. That map is processed through the County planning commission. Once approved, a portion of that neighborhood, maybe about half, is engineered in total detail, and a final map is prepared. This is again processed through the County, mainly the County Engineer, and when approved the map is allowed to be recorded after the improvements are bonded. This is achieved by execution of an agreement with the County called the subdivision agreement. The recordation of the final map allows the parcels to be sold and deeds recorded. The bond ensures to the County and to the buyers that the improvements will be installed as designed.

At the same time, the subdivision is being reviewed by the F.H.A. (Federal Housing Administration) and by the State Real Estate Commissioner. Until F.H.A. approval, loan insurance on the home mortgages is not available. While there would be conventional home mortgage money available without the need for F.H.A. insurance, the mass housing market in the 1960's demanded F.H.A. insured loans. Also, the law required that a Real Estate Commissioner's report be given to each home buyer at the point of sale, so it was necessary that we secure that approval for our builders. This report constitutes complete disclosure of all relevant facts that a buyer might need to make an enlightened decision to buy.

Typically, builders buy land or lots with a down payment, giving a deed of trust back to the seller as security. With a proper bond to protect the seller against liens that might impair the security of the deed of trust, they might build the house and pay the balance on the land sale when the house sale closes. But not in Foster City! We wanted the cash from the sale as quickly as possible, so we structured the transaction for payment in full with the recording of the map. This could be six months before the lots were ready to deliver to the buyer/builder. In addition to bearing the cost of the money invested in lots not yet ready for use, they had the cost of the real estate taxes which started with the transfer of title.

This was a tough requirement and one that separated the strong builder from the weak or, at least, cautious builder. It is testimony to the confidence that they had in us and in Foster City as a market place for their homes that they accepted these difficult terms.

To make it attractive to the builder, we offered the following:
- A delivery schedule that they could reasonably count on.
- A flat lot, approved by the F.H.A. and eligible for a building permit, minimum 55 feet wide with a 1% gradient to the street.
- An aggressive marketing program.
- Reasonably continuous blocks of around twenty lots which would allow economy of scale. They would have liked the sort of big blocks that they were used to in their own developments but we were seeking to avoid that sort of tract look that comes when the same builder builds all the houses.
- Exclusivity; they knew that we planned to limit the number of volume builders to three. This is contrasted with custom builders on the lagoon front lots. More later on this.
- A low land price at the start and thereafter.
- An opportunity to continue with subsequent neighborhoods. Beyond just the first neighborhood, the potential volume was very

large. This promise was not contractual but a good will offer on our part subject only to their continued cooperation and success.

Additional requirements of the builder were:
- A new foundation design. As recommended by Dames & Moore, and designed by structural engineers Rutherford & Chekene, the foundation was to be a reinforced concrete continuous beam foundation that would withstand differential settlement and earthquake. This also became an F.H.A. requirement. At our urging, the County building department made it its requirement as well. We reserved the right to have our own engineers inspect the foundations also but we soon learned that the combined F.H.A. and County inspections were adequate.
- Subjecting their design to our design board for review. The design board was created by the recorded covenants so the control of design was stronger than by just the contractual relationship with the builders. The accepted fashion of tract homes was to put an attractive facade on the front and to cover the other three sites with stucco, ignoring the appearance. While we decided not to try to change that, we did want to approve the front facade and to require that on corner lots, the facade be continued on the side street. (When we get to the lagoon lots which did not involve tract builders, we insisted on architectural treatment all the way around the house.)
- There was to be no racial discrimination.
- The builders were to contribute $250 per house for advertising. This fund, which supplemented what we were spending, was for marketing of Foster City homes generally and Foster City as a place to live. The marketing of their homes specifically was done by them.

We shopped all the top volume builders. If we liked their product and their marketing, we met with them and told them about Foster City. Some were not interested; others liked it but did not like our terms. Of those who felt they could accept it and liked the opportunity, we narrowed it down to those we considered the best. We wanted to select three builders whose offerings were different from each other, in order to have the biggest possible variety of housing types.

Kay Homes, a large and very successful company, owned and run by Irving Kay, built the best valued homes that we saw in Northern California.

He managed to produce the most square footage for the money that we saw and he did it with flair and amenities. He was capable and sophisticated and, while startled by our terms, he understood them and the reason for them, and he accepted them. His partner and superintendent was Leo Leggett, a very able builder.

Our only problem was that we did not like Kay's exterior facades. He assured us that he would cooperate with our design board and produce the architectural look that we wanted. He cooperated fully and later confessed that his product got so much better-looking that, from then on, he hired an architect to advise on all his developments.

Duc & Elliot was a successful home builder in the San Jose area. They built a good looking two story house with a traditional look: colonial, mission and such. We though they would be a good mix with Kay Homes and Eichler, our other selection. Jules Duc was the CEO and was happy to have that segment of the market assigned to him.

One of my memories was when, at the closing of the first sale of lots, just as we were signing the documents and he was about to deliver the check in payment, he said, "Tell me about this Estero District again." It had just dawned on him how much of his tax bill was for Estero.

Eichler Homes was the builder that I wanted the most. I had tremendous admiration for their wonderfully architectural homes. No other builder in America took the design of tract homes to such a contemporary level. They had a national reputation and were especially well known on the Peninsula where they had successfully completed several large developments. Never before had they been a part of someone else's development and required to build their contemporary one story house in and around conventional looking homes. (The other two builders had never built in someone else's development either.)

Eichler Homes was a publicly held corporation led by founder Joe Eichler and his sons Edward (Ned) and Dick. Ned was the man who I dealt with and who bought into the Foster City idea. Their performance in Foster City was as good as I thought it would be. It was after they bought the lots in Neighborhood #3 that the company ran into financial difficulty and was put into receivers' hands. This problem was unrelated to Foster City where they had been very successful and made money but the change effectively prevented them from going forward into further neighborhoods.

Joe Eichler started up again on his own just as our Neighborhood #4 was getting under way. With Eichler Homes out of the picture, I dealt directly with Joe and his new company on this neighborhood where I think some of the best of the Eichlers were built. This was the first time that I got to know the senior Eichler. I recall an incident that occurred as I was driving him and an associate around the neighborhood to look at the lots. We were chatting about something irrelevant to the deal, and the associate spoke of the opportunity to hedge.

Joe said, "What is it to hedge?"

The associate described the process where one invests in something in anticipation of its increasing in value and then negotiates an option to sell (called a "put") to protect himself against its value going the other way.

Joe thought a minute and said, "I don't like that. I wouldn't know which way to hope!"

Among the many honors that were bestowed on Eichler Homes, including many design awards, were awards for their well known policy of totally open housing, meaning that there was no racial discrimination in the neighborhoods which they developed. With one stroke, by bringing Eichler into Foster City, we effectively announced to the world that no one would be denied the opportunity to own a home in Foster City because of race.

We assigned the builders to two general price ranges. We wanted Kay to build the lowest price homes; we expected around $19,000 to $20,000, and the other two about $3000 higher. The opening prices turned out to be about $23,000 for Kay and $26,000 to $27,000 for the other two. The higher prices reflected the confidence of the builders that the market wanted and was willing to pay for that much better house. The price of the lots were $5,500 for Eichler and Duc & Elliot and $5,000 for Kay as long as he stayed well below the other two in price.

The builders started to build their models as soon as they could get on to the site. As the models were going up, the crowds came to see what was going on. Many left their names and asked to be called when sales started. In September, 1963, Kay Homes was the first to open. A sales trailer was moved to the site and before electricity could be hooked up to it, Irving Kay decided to let his salesman start. The first day, a sale was closed every hour until dusk when a cigarette lighter was used to provide the light for the signature of the last sale of the day. Eight sales were made.

There was never a doubt that we had chosen the right builders. The mix of housing was outstanding and the market responded accordingly. All maintained a good rate of sales and construction and eagerly took down the next batch of lots when available. All wanted more lots than they got but knew we were being as fair as possible in dividing them. We resisted the temptation to raise the price of the lots because of the rapid sales rate, and the builders did the same for fear that a higher price would slow their sales behind the rate of the other two builders and might endanger their opportunity to buy the maximum number of lots. The operation was smooth and we remained friends with all three builders throughout.

CHAPTER EIGHT

Leaseholds

WE USED A totally different approach for the homes to be offered on the lagoon front. These lots were special and deserved special treatment. Because the homes were extremely visible from the water, and because just being on the water made them more desirable, we wanted to bring custom designers and custom builders into Foster City. The problem was that the obviously higher price that the lagoon front justified, combined with the higher price that the custom builder had to charge, put the price into a range that we feared could not be sustained. There were homes in upper Hillsborough on half acre lots, being offered for $45,000.

Our solution was to bring to Foster City that which we had a lot of experience with in Hawaii, the long term ground lease. By leasing rather than selling the land, we were able to have custom builders deliver a home for $35,000.

The lease was drawn with great care. Whereas the Hawaii market understood leaseholds, the California market did not. In Hawaii, the lease was typically for 55 years with the first rent reopening in 15 to 25 years. Our lease was for 75 years with the first reopening in 30 years. The reopening is an event when the rent steps up according to a formula in the lease. Early drafts were circulated to lenders for comment. Their suggestions were incorporated into the lease to make it more financeable.

The "Captain's House" at the end of Flying Cloud Isle, was the first home built in Foster City. It was designed by Germano Milano and was built by Ruben White, a prominent custom builder, who had built numerous homes in Hillsborough. The house was not for sale but was used as a show house to introduce the custom program. Fox & Carskaden, a prominent local realty firm, was given the listing to sell this program and operated out of this house. The program went well and 227 were sold from 1964 through 1966.

The tight money crisis of 1966 put an end to the lease program. From then on, lots were sold to builders and an offer was made to all the lessees to sell them their lots. The price to lessees ranged from $7500 to $16,000 per lot, depending on the amount of ground rent called for in the lease. 9 lessees bought their lots, bringing the total remaining to 218.

The next effort was in the mid 80's when 69 leased lots were sold, ranging in prices from $43,000 to $68,000. This was a time of inflation, particularly as to real estate values, and especially in Foster City. For this reason, we discontinued sales.

As we approached the years when the rents reopened (1993, 1994, and 1995), we became concerned that the implications of the reopening were vastly misunderstood. We had seen cases of leased properties changing hands and not even the brokers understanding how to evaluate a leasehold. We were convinced that the real estate disclosure laws were being violated, though one would think that a buyer of a leasehold would read the lease that he was assuming and note that the rent would soon increase. There were some cases where the home owner did not know that he was on a leasehold; in such a case, the mortgage lender was paying the ground rent and the amount was so nominal, perhaps $60 a month, that it was overlooked.

In March of 1989 we wrote a letter to all the lessees to alert them to what the new rent might be. We said that current appraisals indicated land values ranged from $270,000 to $320,000, and that the new ground rent, at 5%, would be around $15,000 a year. The letter caused a sensation. It was front page news in *The San Mateo Times* for days.

The leaseholders formed a committee and attorneys were hired to consider their remedies. The result was Measure E which would create a rent control ordinance, limited to rents on land only. The city council refused to adopt it, so, with 4471 signatures gathered, it was placed on the Foster City ballot. There were only 149 leases at this point. Such an ordinance, if enacted, would guarantee litigation based on interference in contractual relationships. It was soundly defeated at the polls, 5710 to 2847.

At this time we offered to all the lessees a life-of-lease option to buy the land at fair market value, less a discount of 32% with the discount going down by 1% a year. In time, all the leaseholders accepted the amendment and, eventually, everyone bought their land . . . . except one person, but that's another story.

T. JACK FOSTER, JR.

CHAPTER NINE

Non-discrimination

TODAY, NO-ONE UNDER the age of 50 can imagine that a person could be denied the right to buy a house, simply because his skin was black. Prior to 1960, discrimination was the rule more than not. Martin Luther King, Jr.'s famous march on Washington was in 1963.

The Rumford Fair Housing Act was passed by the State of California in 1963 and prohibited discrimination in the sale of housing. Proposition 14 qualified for the ballot in 1964, and passed with 65% of the vote, effectively voiding the Rumford Act. It ruled that anyone could sell or rent his property to anyone he wanted to, and the State could not interfere. Remarkable! The people of California voted overwhelmingly for the right to continue discrimination in housing. The U.S. Supreme Court voided Proposition 14 in 1966.

Even while the Rumford Act was in effect, it was winked at and widely but slyly evaded in many residential areas. Many builders feared that integration of their development would mean the loss of sales to the white majority, though Eichler did not have that experience. Many people feared that the presence of a black neighbor would affect the value of their homes. Some places had restrictive covenants prohibiting the sale of homes to minorities. These still exist in older properties but the courts have held that they are illegal and unenforceable.

In addition, President John Kennedy ordered that F.H.A. not allow discrimination in any development in which F.H.A. was participating. I recall receiving a notice from F.H.A. in Washington that we were specifically prohibited from noting in any record of any kind the race of a prospective or actual buyer. A year or so later I received another communication from F.H.A. in Washington asking me to fill out a questionnaire to tell them the numbers of buyers in each of several categories, all racial. I took joy in writing across the front of the questionnaire, "Information not known."

The Civil Rights Act was finally passed by the U.S, Congress in 1964 under the leadership of President Lyndon Johnson.

As the civil rights movement was building, we decided that our position in Foster City should be unequivocal. There must be no discrimination in the sale or rental of houses. Once it was made clear, and the presence of Eichler helped, there was no need to discuss it any more. I don't think that sales in Foster City were affected in the slightest and, in fact, our market was broadened when minorities learned that they did not have to play games in the purchase of a house in Foster City.

Chinese American were among the earliest buyers in Foster City. I think that was because Eichler advertised in the Chinese Times newspaper in San Francisco and drew a lot of interest from those ads.

In about 1965, I first met Mercedes Rosen. "Mike" was a beautiful African-American lady, married to a white Jewish man, who lived in Foster City with their two attractive children of this mixed racial marriage. She came into my office, after making an appointment. She acknowledged her pleasure at living in Foster City and her ability to buy her home without the slightest hint of discrimination, but came to ask us to do more. She asked that our advertising include photographs of blacks. It so happens that we were completing work on the first brochure that used color photographs rather than art work. This was to be a large run and would be the main all purpose Foster City brochure. There was a photograph, already scheduled for inclusion, which showed children playing on the beach in the bathing suits. Some of the children were black. She said, "This is perfect. It is natural, not posed, and shows a lot of skin." She thanked me and left.

She was in the travel business and a few years later decided to open her own travel agency. She rented space in our building and did a thriving business. We became good friends and she took care of all of our travel requirements. I hated to see her retire and move out of the building. She and her husband eventually left Foster City entirely as they moved away for retirement. A few years ago I received a phone call from Mike. I had not heard from her for a long time. She said that she had an illness and did not have much longer to live and was calling as many of her old friends who she could locate to say good-bye. We had a wonderful chat about old times. I sent her some flowers and then, a few weeks later tried to call her. I learned that she had died.

Ike Tribble was a noted leader in the black community and was a consultant to Mills College in Oakland and to other institutions in matters of race. He was a frequent speaker in the Bay Area. My wife, Pat, heard him speak at a meeting of the Junior League of San Francisco when he said that in spite of the Rumford Act there was still widespread discrimination in the communities of the Bay Area, except for one, and that was Foster City. I was told that he repeated this in other forums.

In 1996, we were presented a trophy inscribed:

To the Foster Family
With Gratitude For Bold Leadership
In A Civil Rights Cause By Embracing
Diversity in Housing
San Mateo Branch NAACP
Marie Davis, President

Marie Davis is another early Foster City resident whom I knew. She is a charming lady with a beautiful voice who has sung in many venues including the Star Spangled Banner for the start of Giants baseball games. She has long been a good active citizen and involved in many activities in Foster City. I am grateful for this salute from her and the NAACP.

CHAPTER TEN

Community Relations

ANOTHER AREA OF public relations that commanded our attention was within the growing Foster City community itself. There the problems were completely different. It turned out that our co-ownership of the *Foster City Progress,* the only newspaper in town until 1972, was a marvelous tool for communicating with the new residents. While it truly started as a potential profit making venture per George McQueen's suggestion, it served as a way of communicating with the residents and at the same time, building enthusiasm for their new town—which is what a newspaper is supposed to do. We tried to keep the paper fair and objective. When we wanted to present our position as developer of the city, we would use a column with a by-line.

Our whole organization was sensitive to the Foster City community. We made special efforts to be aware of their problems and to deal with them as best we could. Early on, the most difficult problem was just the construction environment. With no trees or buildings acting as wind breaks, the wind in spring could be fierce. (We referred to them as our sailing winds.) The pioneer residents were good natured about the blowing dirt and put up with a lot as we did our best to deal with it. The loose soil from the fill and construction operations created days that were pretty unpleasant. The biggest problem came from what is now the town center. After trying different methods of holding down the blowing soil, we finally gained some control by installing parallel rows of low fencing similar to what is used to encourage snow to drift. We also seeded the soil to attempt to get plant growth to cover it.

The early residents organized to deal with their problems and their organization became the Foster City Community Association (FCCA). One of the early issues had to do with the decision of the elementary school district to eliminate school bus service to Foster City. The residents were aware that we had offered to donate to the school district the first school site, and came to us to suggest that we make that offer contingent on the continuance of bus service. We did as they suggested and the school board capitulated and agreed to continue the bus service. Generally speaking, we enjoyed a good relationship with the early residents.

One day, Senator Richard Dolwig informed us that a young lawyer, Wayne McFadden by name, had approached him to ask his advice about moving into Foster City for the purpose of establishing a legal practice. Dolwig was himself a practicing lawyer. He said that he advised McFadden that he thought Foster City was going to be very successful and a good place to start a practice. Then he said that McFadden was very ambitious and was apt to be a problem for us.

Earnest Wilson, the senior partner in Wilson, Morton, & Lynch, the bond attorneys for the Estero District also warned about McFadden. McFadden had worked in that office as he sought to learn the municipal finance field.

When the FCCA next came to see us about something or another, we met Wayne McFadden for the first time.

The predictions quickly turned out to be accurate as we saw McFadden "view with alarm" the debt and the debt service of the Estero District. It became the stepping stone to his control of FCCA, the Estero District, the incorporation of Foster City, his election as mayor, and then, one year later, his resignation as mayor and assumption of the District's litigation business, much of which litigation he himself had initiated. Thus, in a few short years, he had the legal practice that he sought.

In the beginning, for a short time, we thought we might be able to negotiate with him. When I say "him" of course I mean the FCCA. Occasionally we tried an end run by talking with some other leader in the FCCA only to learn that whatever agreement we might have been able to secure was reversed when McFadden got hold of him. We realized that an agreement could only be made with McFadden. The few in the FCCA leadership. like Jim Duffelmeyer, who finally stood up to McFadden, were turned out.

As we made concessions to McFadden, he was back with more demands. We cynically began to label our concessions, like: a one day concession meant we figured it bought us peace for one day, or, in the case of a really big concession, a two week concession. Perhaps it would last that long. Finally, we realized that he wanted total control and he knew that to get it he had to get rid of us.

The FCCA knew that land sales were extremely important to us. They realized that anything they could do to prevent a sale would impose pressure on us. One case involved a zoning application. It was for a townhouse project, which consisted of connected units at the density of ten per acre. This compares to twenty per acre for garden apartments. We had a developer who would buy the land when the zoning was confirmed. Jim Duffelmeyer, president of FCCA, appeared before the County Board of Supervisors to ask that the zoning not be granted. I was dumbfounded to hear him say that such a development "represented future slums for Foster City."

Considering that there were already successful townhouse developments in neighborhoods one and two, I wondered what the FCCA members in those projects thought of that judgment. At any rate, the zoning which had been approved by the County Planning Commission was denied by the Board of Supervisors under pressure from the FCCA. We lost the sale. Subsequently, the same parcel was zoned by the new city council of Foster City without argument and the sale was made by Centex, who had taken our position by that time. That council consisted of the same people who opposed the zoning when it was before the County.

We also were aware that members of the FCCA talked to our banks about us and while there is no evidence that anything ensued, certainly we knew that the banks were concerned about the attitude of the Foster City residents—as well as they might be. One ploy that was considered by the FCCA insiders was that they all put their homes on the market as a public protest to our opposition to turning control of the Estero District over to them. They backed away from this out of fear that their houses would be sold.

Our opposition to McFadden, at all levels, the state, the county and even in Foster City, was based on our obligation that we felt we had to successfully complete the project. Paramount were the interests of those early residents who bought into Foster City. We also felt that it was vital to consider as well, the interests of those who bought Estero bonds, of the industrial and commercial interests, the banks and other lenders and other investors in Foster City. I could safely and comfortably say to the political leaders, as I did in public at times, that if McFadden and the FCCA were allowed to have their way and take total control of the Estero District, Foster City and the Estero District could fail. I believe that just as intensely today, as I write this. It is to the credit of the elected officials at the time, that they declined to give them the immediate control that they wanted.

The Estero Board consisted of three people elected by the land owner. In the first election, Dad, as general partner, cast the vote on behalf of T. Jack Foster & Sons, who owned almost all of the land. Dick Grant, Bill Innes and George Shannon were put on the Board. Shortly thereafter, Dick Grant chose to resign and it was decided to invite the County Board of Supervisors to nominate someone to look out for the broader interest. Chris Olmo, a local contractor, was suggested and he was thereupon elected to the Board and named chairman.

The FCCA wanted the law changed to have all three elected by residents. They even sought from the state attorney general a ruling that the "one man/one vote" doctrine handed down by the Supreme Court be applied to the Estero District. The Attorney General refused.

As they sought from Assemblyman Leo Ryan his introduction of an amendment to the Estero Act to give them control, I met also with Ryan to fashion a compromise that would give us time. We came up with the concept of enlarging the Board to five members with two elected by residents, two elected on a land owner vote, and the fifth appointed by the Board of Supervisors. Over time, the appointed seat would become elective by residents and then after that, all five would become similarly elective. Ryan offered that to the FCCA and they reluctantly accepted it. The amendment, introduced by Assemblyman John Knox, passed the legislature and was signed into law.

The first election of the enlarged board was held in November, 1967, and Dr. Charles Monahan, president of FCCA, and Wayne McFadden were elected to the two "resident" seats. I don't think that five minutes of peace or civility ensued at any time thereafter until the residents took total control at the end of 1969. The Board of Supervisors asked Chris Olmo to continue as their appointee until a decision was made as to who would hold that seat. FCCA were fighting to get another resident appointed and I was urging that the appointment go to a fair and objective outsider. The newest member of the Board of Supervisors was Bob St. Clair. He offered to accept the appointment on the Estero board and be that fair and objective outsider. FCCA vigorously opposed it and after a time he withdrew. The Board eventually appointed Allen Beaumont, a Burlingame resident and vice president of Glore Forgan/William R. Staats, a municipal bond firm which had dealt with Estero Bonds. He put up with the turmoil for less than a year and then resigned. The County Board then appointed Alvin Potter, an attorney and a Foster City resident. He was not in the FCCA so was just as unacceptable to the FCCA as was Beaumont.

Potter was elected chairman and in a famous episode when he was trying to conduct the meeting of the Board, McFadden continually interrupted and would not allow the meeting to go forward. Potter ordered him to be silent or be arrested. He continued the disruption so Potter had him arrested. This, of course, made the headlines of the local press. The County Attorney prosecuted, McFadden was found innocent, and sued the Estero District for $100,000 for false arrest. He settled for $5,000, his first profit from his Foster City involvement.

While we knew Beaumont as a result of his company's investment in Estero bonds, we had never met Al Potter. He offered his services and brought to the Board a fairness and objectivity that we wanted but that McFadden and Monahan did not. The County Board saw him as a good appointment because he had no prior involvement plus the fact that he was a Foster City resident, something the FCCA was clamoring for. It turned out that what they were really clamoring for was an appointment of one of their own.

Eventually, in 1969, when McFadden, et al, took total control of the Estero District, enough good things had happened along the way that Foster City was stronger and more able to withstand the vagaries of their operation of the district. I was not sure that we were, however. It was clear, early on, that they planned to push to incorporation as a city. This was not unreasonable to us except for the fact that incorporation would give them total control, including zoning. Since we had already experienced their approach to zoning when they fought, as FCCA, the zoning of the townhouse land for the purpose of hurting our cash flow, we knew that we were unlikely to survive incorporation under their control. And their control of the city seemed rather absolute. We knew of residents who disagreed with them and their tactics, but who had more to do with their lives than to take them on. So we had to face the fact that the new town would be run by the same people then running the Estero District.

Our choices were few and difficult. One choice was to sell our position. This was what McFadden and friends wanted. If we were unable to achieve a sale, we would have no choice but to block incorporation, and we still owned enough land to do that. This was not a happy alternative.

CHAPTER ELEVEN

1966-1970

A S THE ESTERO Municipal Improvement District was evolving into total resident control, and additionally, incorporation, I pause to recount what else was going on in the development of Foster City.

The land fill had settled down into a smooth and efficient operation with the 10 millionth cubic yard put in place by the end of 1965. Home sales and apartment rentals continued apace with the population estimated at 5,000 by October, 1966. Some industrial sales took place and church congregations got under way, usually meeting in schools.

Foster City was not immune from the vagaries of the bigger economic picture. August, 1966, was the first serious tight money of the decade. Interest rates shot up, loans became hard to get, and panic of sorts set in. A large garden apartment project which was approved, financed, and on which we had started construction, had to be cancelled because the construction financing was cancelled by Well Fargo. Home sales came to a complete halt for a period of over thirty days—the first such halt in Foster City's history. It was a national crisis. We stopped all advertising during the crisis.

It was at this time, 1966, that Walter Cooper, a resident on one of the waterfront leasehold lots, filed a class action suit attacking the legality of the Estero District and suing the Foster family for $30 million. It was a suit so without merit that it was eventually dismissed on demurer without leave to amend. (The "without leave to amend" part was the court's way of saying that the failure to make a case was so complete that the plaintiff was not permitted to amend and refile it.) But that decision took many months, and then Cooper filed other suits and appealed each decision that he lost, and he lost them all. Finally, in October, 1969, the Supreme Count refused to hear his appeal.

The damage of the lawsuits was enormous. The Estero District was prevented for a time of issuing bonds, so the dredging had to be halted. The municipal bond community was confused and concerned as was the banking community who were financing homes and commercial enterprises. Even the FCCA with their own agenda was troubled by this legal action and filed suit to try to stop it.

The municipal finance world bought and sold bonds depending on their having a legal opinion attached which, in effect, said that everything related to the legal issuance of the bonds had been examined and found to be in order. A legal opinion on the Estero bonds had been written by the Wilson firm in San Mateo who represented the district. But for widest marketability of the bonds, it was important to have a "marketable" opinion, that is, an opinion by a nationally known attorney so widely respected that there could be no doubt about the legality of every aspect of the issuance of the bonds. Whatever risk there might be in the investment, it would not be in their legality. The number of such firms with such a reputation is extremely limited.

The district was able to secure such an opinion from New York City attorney, John N. Mitchell, of Caldwell, Trimble and Mitchell. (This is the same Mitchell who later became Nixon's Attorney General, and was disgraced for his efforts in support of Nixon in Watergate. In fact, before Nixon became president, Mitchell merged his firm into Nixon's. The opinions on the later Estero bonds were by Mitchell with the firm of Nixon, Mudge, Rose, Guthrie and Alexander.) Mitchell's opinion was not available on the earliest bonds, but when he agreed to do it, it made a huge difference in the acceptance of the bonds.

Now, with the Cooper suit, the legality of the district was being questioned. The legal opinions had to be withheld while Mitchell and his associates examined the matter. Bond sales stopped, so the fill operation had to be stopped as well. Finally, Mitchell was able to issue an opinion which took note of the litigation and that he had examined it and was of the opinion that it was without merit. With that, bond sales resumed.

In summer of 1965, in what was thought to be a routine surgery, my Father's cancer was discovered which was to end his life on March 15, 1968.

The Republic National Bank of Dallas, Texas, the 20th largest bank in the country and the biggest in Texas, which was our lead bank since the early 1950's, became concerned and refused to issue additional credit.

It was apparent that we needed a reliable source of money. I knew of the relationship which the James Rouse Company had with the Connecticut General Life Insurance Company, where Connecticut General put up all the money for the new town, Columbia, Maryland, in exchange for half interest. We approached them to see if we could make a similar deal. After a careful analysis, they agreed to do so providing that the present creditors would extend the debt. Understandably Connecticut General did not want to advance money for payment of debt. This would be Republic Bank, Wells Fargo, and the Schilling Estate Company/Leslie Salt Company who had the seller's deed of trust. Wells and Schilling agreed but Republic Bank would not agree and said that for us to "give away" half the deal was too much to pay. They said that they would consider taking a partnership role of some sort. They sent Arthur Anderson & Co., auditors, to examine our pro forma and projections and after a number of months, Anderson recommended against it and the Bank declined to participate. At this point the Connecticut General connection was lost.

There can be no doubt that our single greatest mistake made in the development of Foster City was the decision to finance the ongoing operation with a reliance on bank support and cash flow from land sales. My Dad had always been successful with development loans from Republic National Bank of Dallas. The difference this time, fully understood by us as well as by the bank was the long range aspect of the development plus the enormous size. The senior officers of the bank who made the commitment had retired, and while the success of the development was gratifying, the problems of the bad publicity from the FCCA agitation and the Cooper suits and the money crunch created a loss of confidence. Had a deal like the Connecticut General deal been made at the outset, we could have maintained control without having to worry about ongoing cash flow problems.

Centex Corp. was a large developer/home builder based in Dallas, in the Republic Bank building. Republic Bank sought to have Centex buy us out of Foster City. We went to Dallas in April, 1969, to start negotiations. It was evident that that they felt that they were negotiating from a position of power, what with the bank pressing us. The negotiations went poorly. They would state their position on a matter then add, "That is non-negotiable."

And then, suddenly, FHA declared a moratorium on Foster City and Redwood Shores. The moratorium stemmed from criticism leveled at FHA by a congressional oversight committee which claimed that FHA had been approving developments too easily without adequate consideration of the geologic risks. Specifically, they had failed to consider USGS warnings about earthquake risks in Foster City and Redwood Shores.

This meant that, until it was resolved, FHA would not issue a subdivision report on any development within those two communities. Where a report had been issued by them, it would be honored and the home loans within those approved areas would continue to be eligible for loan insurance. It hit at a critical time for Redwood Shores as they were just getting started. Foster City had enough neighborhoods approved that production there was not affected, though eventually, it could be a problem. It was enough to spook Centex who ended negotiations.

During this interim, some good things started to happen. We completed the sale of a sizable amount of land to L. B. Nelson, a major developer of apartments. The Cooper litigation finally ended—for good. We sold the Commodore Apartments. The Kaufman & Broad townhouse project was a huge success. We completed a major transaction with Boise Cascade for industrial land. The population of Foster City hit 10,000.

With the lifting of the FHA moratorium in May, 1970, plus the other favorable happenings, Centex called to renew negotiations. I attached three conditions: (1) the price went up by $500,000; (2) all negotiations were to be in California; (3) the word "non-negotiable" was never to be uttered. They immediately agreed and negotiations resumed—in California. A contract was signed in October, 1970, and the development was turned over to Centex.

So our decade-long role in Foster City had ended. It was sad for me in some respects as I looked forward to pushing it toward completion, though a viable, ongoing community is never completed—it continues to evolve. There could be no doubt but that it was the best thing that could happen to the Foster family. We were free of debt, free of litigation and struggle. I knew that, though Centex had a clean slate and a good reputation, and was welcomed by the community leaders in power, the honeymoon would be short.

Having taken control of the Estero District, the FCCA leaders secured a petition from the residents asking for incorporation. There was a public hearing before the County Board of Supervisors. The case for incorporation was made and the public hearing was closed, whereupon Supervisor Bill Werder made the motion that an election be called in Foster City and that, "if the voters approve, the area would be incorporated as San Mateo County's newest city and it would be called Foster City." As soon as he heard the motion, McFadden leapt to his feet shouting, "Mr. Chairman, Mr. Chairman." He was informed that the public hearing had been closed and he was not allowed to speak. The motion passed. While leaving the meeting, he was heard to mutter, "We can change the name later." The election was held, passed, and incorporation occurred in 1971. Turmoil reigned but the Fosters were not a part of it.

We had retained some income properties (the leased lots, Port O' Call shopping center, our office complex which included the Wells Fargo Bank) but we were, at that point, complete outsiders, observing the goings-on of the new City dealing with the continued development, primarily with Centex, but also with L. B. Nelson, and other developers, now in the industrial park. The next six or seven years, before matters settled down, have been recorded by others but it involved a refusal by Centex to pay taxes, the resultant financial crises, then litigation. The Corps of Engineers refused to allow the ongoing land fill, which resulted in a Congressional hearing in Foster City. While we were not particularly affected, our ownership of the *Foster City Progress* allowed me, via signed front page columns, to comment on some of these matters. I don't know how valuable they were, but they were the only public observations with that point of view. And it helped me to get it off of my chest.

I am now going to reveal a long held secret. (You read it here first.) We had a small interest in the Centex profit on Foster City. In 1981, my brother, Dick, and I flew to Dallas for the purpose of picking up a check. I met, for the first time, Jack MacDonald, president of Centex. He apologized for not having met us before but explained, in his ongoing dealings with the Foster City leaders, they kept questioning if the Fosters had a profit share with them. He denied that we did, but it helped to say that he had never met us before. There was no doubt in his mind that, as difficult was it was to deal with them, it would have been near impossible had they known that the Fosters would have shared in some small fashion with the results of an agreement. Frankly, for most of the decade of the seventies, it appeared to Centex that their involvement was going to produce a loss but, at the end of their inventory, inflation had set in and the last land sales were very profitable.

CHAPTER TWELVE

In Retrospect

F ROM THIS YEAR, 2012, I look back 54 years to when my Dad, my brothers and I first saw the land that became Foster City. It was the beginning of twelve remarkable years which turned difficult, until 1970, when we stepped aside and Centex came in to finish the development

For those years following 1970, we continued to maintain an office in Foster City, at the same place, 1015 East Hillsdale Blvd., across the street from the library. My brother, Dick, and I continued to operate the family partnership; my brother, Bob, withdrew to pursue other interests. At this point we had no role to play in the development except that we were observers. We managed our income properties in Foster City, and at the same time, pursued other opportunities. We developed a twelve story luxury condominium in San Mateo, on Third Avenue. There were two penthouses, one on each end of the twelfth floor. Dick took one and I took the other, moving in, in 1980.

Eventually, matters settled down in Foster City, as the electorate put in a council which installed a proper city management team and allowed them to manage. I liked what I saw in their operation of the city, but I did not know what our standing might be with the council. Then, a member of the library committee asked us to consider commissioning a statue of our Dad for installation at the library. We felt very honored, and started looking for a sculptor. Then, it dawned on us that we had better proceed cautiously. I could foresee a community rhubarb over whether a statue of the man who loaded all that debt on the community should be placed in the library. So we told the library committee that, before proceeding further, we would like for the city council to approve. The city council not only approved, but said they would rather have the statue in front of the new city hall which they were about to build.

My brother, Dick, and I went to work, found the sculptor, Bruce Wolfe, and commissioned a statue. We put together a stack of photographs, including old family snapshots, to give him an idea of what Dad looked like. The result is remarkable. He could not have captured Dad's likeness better if Dad had posed in person.

The city had paid five outstanding architectural firms to submit conceptual plans for a new city hall. The winner would be given the design contract. A requirement of the specifications was to include the statue in the plan. The five models were on display, and I went to look at them. I was delighted to see, in each model, a tiny statue, at scale, a fraction of an inch high.

The statue was completed long before the city was ready for it, so we put the statue in the lobby of our office building. There it stood until the city was ready for its permanent installation. To this day, I like to drop by city hall to see the statue. I like to go on a Sunday or holiday when no one is around.

In 2000 we moved our office out of Foster City when the building was torn down to make way for the bigger office complex. We eventually sold all of our Foster City income properties.

My ties to Foster City remained just as strong. All three of my children moved there with their families. Two are still there. Most of my grandchildren have lived there, some of them practically all of their lives. I have attended several Bowditch graduation events at the Ryan Park amphitheater.

I have a 21 foot electric boat, a Duffy, which is tied up at my son's house. It has given me great pleasure through the years, touring the Foster City lagoon.

For years, my late wife, Pat, and I went to Foster City to walk our dog, either on the levee or in Ryan Park. Today, I frequently take the dog to one of the remote parks where I can let her run free, as I sit on a bench and enjoy.

I never miss a show at Hillbarn Theater, which my daughter, Lee, has run for twelve years. It is the oldest community theater in California, having started in San Mateo in the 1940's. In time, it moved to San Carlos. In 1964, I was invited to a meeting of local citizens who were trying to raise money to buy a site in Burlingame for the construction of a theater.

I thought, "I can do better than that." I approached my Dad and brothers and suggested that we donate a site in Foster City. They agreed and the rest is history.

Through the years, people have made a point of telling me how much they have loved living in Foster City. This has pleased me very much. I felt very complimented that they wanted to tell me that. Another story that has come to me is the young married couple who chose to live in Foster City because they grew up there, and their parents and their grandparents live there. Think of that! Three generations!

The improvement bonds which were issued to raise the money to develop Foster City have been paid off. I see Foster City being acknowledged as one of the best places to live; as being one of the soundest financially during these difficult times when some cities have taken bankruptcy; as having perhaps the best parks in the county and the best streets. It has made me very proud.

T. JACK FOSTER, JR.

AUTOBIOGRAPHY

T. Jack Foster, Jr.

FIRST—ABOUT MY DAD: T. Jack Foster was born in Mineral Wells, Texas, on April 18, 1902. He was the youngest of eleven children, consisting of eight from the first marriage of his father, Thomas Jefferson Foster, and three from his second marriage, entered into after his first wife died.

Thomas Jefferson Foster, born in 1841, was named for his father, born in 1805. Both of them fought in the Civil War. Dad was named for his father and grandfather, making him Thomas Jefferson Foster III. His mother died in 1906 and his father died in 1907, making him an orphan at age 5.

He was always called Jack for some reason that he didn't know. He always said he thought it was because he had big ears. At any rate, as he grew up, it never occurred to him that he had a different name. Eventually, as an adult in the business world when he encountered another Jack Foster in town he realized that, to avoid confusion, he needed an initial, so he started using the "T" for Thomas, in front of his name. He named his first born son (me) Thomas Jack Foster, Jr., who did the same for his son, Thomas Jack Foster III, who did the same, Thomas Jack Foster IV. (One could say that he is Thomas J. Foster VI in a line dating back over 200 years.)

The five year old orphan and his two brothers aged 7 and 8, were raised by their half sisters. The eight older half siblings ranged in age from 18 to 41. One sister, married but without children, lived in Dallas and kept the boys during the school months. In the summer they lived with another sister in Coalgate, Oklahoma, who was married to a rancher. Growing up on a working ranch was hard work, but it contributed immeasurably, and positively, to the sort of people they became.

Dad followed his brothers to the University of Oklahoma at Norman. He had no money so he immediately started looking for a way of earning it He got a deal with a local cleaning establishment to pick up cleaning from the dorms and fraternities and delivering the clean clothes back. He somehow managed this from a motorcycle. This evolved quickly—while still in college—to building his own cleaning establishment, which he called University Cleaners.

He married my Mother, Gladys Hutchins, from Davis, Oklahoma, in 1922. He was twenty and she was twenty two. I came along in 1928, brother Bob in 1931, and brother Dick in 1934.

Dad entered law school at the University of Oklahoma, and, as a business man in Norman, became interested and active in local government. So active, in fact, that he ran for and was elected mayor of Norman, receiving national publicity as a "school-boy mayor." His first step as a developer was in 1939 when he built the 64 unit Norman Courts Motel. This was a motel with everything a hotel had. It was unique for the times and was honored by Duncan Hines, noted hotel critic, who called it one of the five best in the U.S.

I worked most summers of my life, usually for Dad. When he was building the motel he had the carpenters erect a stand for me (age 9 or 10) to go into the business of selling soda pop to the workers. My Mother showed me how to keep books where I would enter the daily revenue. When I bought soda pop and ice, I entered that. Getting a little bored, I hired a neighborhood friend to work for me. I paid 10 cents a day and entered that cost in my books.

In the summers which followed I had a variety of jobs at the motel, from gardener to maid to room clerk.

In time, Dad invested in a pumice mine in New Mexico with an office in Albuquerque. Pumice is a volcanic rock which is very porous and was being mined for use as an aggregate in concrete in place of gravel. It allowed the concrete to be very light weight with a strong insulation factor for use in very specific circumstances. The pumice was loaded into open freight cars and shipped to concrete block manufacturers and ready mix plants in 15 different states. I worked in the office in the summer of 1946 after I

T. JACK FOSTER, JR.

graduated from high school and again the next summer after my freshman year at the University of Oklahoma.

I was having difficulty choosing a major so Dad persuaded me to stay out of school for a year and continue to run that office. So at age 19, I was living alone in Albuquerque and managing this small office. We were preparing bills of lading for the shipment of pumice aggregate, responding to inquiries from customers and potential customers, paying bills, etc. I was dictating letters to a secretary.

In 1948, I returned to O.U where I majored in Business Administration. I graduated in 1951. While there I edited the *Sooner Yearbook*. I was inducted into Phi Eta Sigma and Beta Gamma Sigma honorary societies, received the Pe-et award as one of ten outstanding senior men, and was in Who's Who in American Colleges and Universities. I was a member of Phi Delta Theta fraternity.

Having earned a commission through ROTC in the Air Force, I was called to active duty and assigned to Kirtland Air Force Base in—Albuquerque! I was a finance officer in the Special Weapons Command of the Air Force. This command represented the Air Force in the development of the atomic bomb. Our base had personnel on temporary duty at Indian Springs Air Force Base in Nevada. One of my assignments was to fill a satchel with cash and to go there to service the pay records of our personnel. I was prepared to make cash advances when needed. While there, I got to witness two tests of atomic bombs.

Released in 1953, I went immediately to Honolulu, Hawaii, where I went to work for my Dad's partner, Bill Likins. They had formed a partnership in about 1948 for the purpose of developing and building housing for the military under the National Housing Act. At various military installations the Federal Housing Administration would call for proposals from qualified developers to build housing for rent. Likins Foster & Associates were successful in several locations around the country. Near Pearl Harbor we were selected to build 500 houses. This development was under way when I arrived.

Two years later, Dad bought out Likins and formed the family partnership, T. Jack Foster & Sons. He told me that he wanted me to take over the Hawaii operation. I panicked and tried to demur. He insisted that I do it, that he would be back and forth frequently. He said to me, "Do you know how farmers back in Oklahoma taught their kids to swim?" The answer: "They threw them in the water." I asked if any of the farmers ever let their kids drown. He assured me that they did not and that he wouldn't let me drown. He promised me a first class construction superintendant so I wouldn't have to worry about that. So I took over. I was 27.

That 500 house development grew to 750. When the houses were starting to be completed, we offered them for rent to military personnel as required, but quickly found that the military had either miscalculated the need or else it had changed. At any rate, we learned that there was no market for rentals. With the permission of the FHA, we commenced a program to sell the houses. We eventually built 250 more houses for sale in that development. We acquired land nearby which we got approved by the City and built and sold 500 more. This development was called Foster Village and was a step above the first one.

There were other housing developments in Hawaii which we joint ventured with another builder. Then we started the 25 story Foster Tower in Waikiki, a residential building.

My life at about this time had to do with Foster City which is what this book is about. So I moved to California in 1960 with my wife, the former Patricia Chesnut, and our two children, daughter Lee and son Jack. Son Mark was born in 1962. Pat died in November, 2010, after almost 57 years of marriage.

As for my community activities:

I served as President of Comprehensive Health Planning Council of San Mateo County, Treasurer and Board member of the Bay Area Comprehensive Health Planning Council and first Chairman of the Health Network Consortium of San Mateo County. I was President of San Mateo County Economic Development Association (SAMCEDA) and the Junior Statesman Foundation. I was President and served on the Board of Trustees and the distribution committee of the Peninsula Community Foundation. I was chairman of the Housing & Homeless Task Force. I served on the Boards of the Governmental Research Council, the San Mateo County

Arts Council, the Family Service Agency of San Mateo County, Easter Seal Society, American Red Cross of San Mateo County, San Mateo County Chapter of the American Cancer Society, and the San Francisco Ballet Association. I was a Commissioner of the Human Resources Commission of the City of San Mateo, and served as chairman in 1996. I was a board member of the San Mateo County Historical Association. I am a past president of the San Mateo Rotary Club.

My wife, Pat, also did a lot of community service. One year, we were jointly honored as "The Volunteers of the Year" by the Volunteer Center of San Mateo County.

While in Honolulu, I was president of the Home Builders Association of Hawaii, Chairman of the Mid Pacific Housing Conference and Chairman of the Mayor's Special Committee on Housing for Displaced Persons.

www.ingramcontent.com/pod-product-compliance
Lightning Source LLC
Chambersburg PA
CBHW020334290526
45785CB00005B/2009